FRANCIS FRITH'S THROUGH THE RHONDDA TO PONTYPRIDD

LIVING MEMORIES

JOHN A MILNES AND JULIA SKINNER

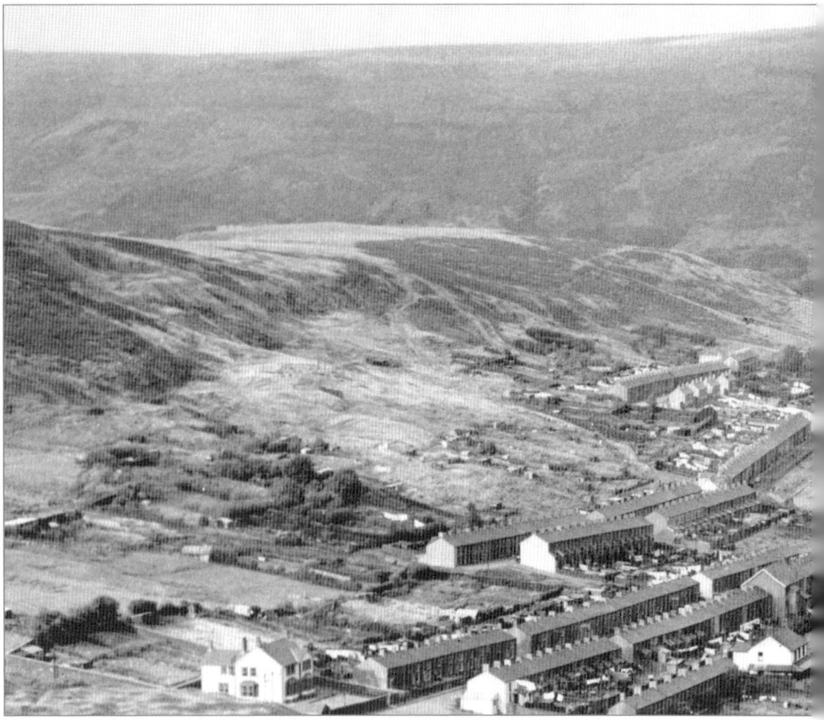

FRANCIS FRITH'S

PHOTOGRAPHIC MEMORIES

THROUGH THE RHONDDA TO PONTYPRIDD

LIVING MEMORIES

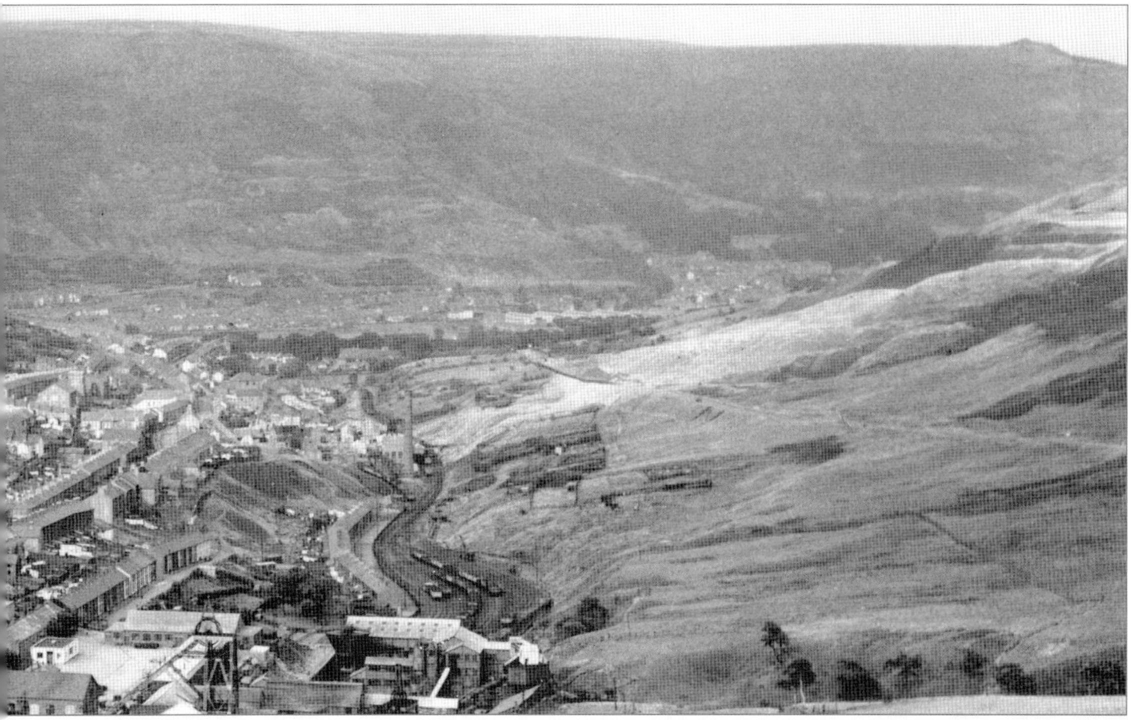

JOHN A MILNES AND JULIA SKINNER

THE FRANCIS FRITH COLLECTION®

First published in paperback in the United Kingdom in 2003
by The Francis Frith Collection as Rhondda Valley Living Memories
ISBN: 1-85937-653-3

Revised edition published in paperback in 2011
as Through the Rhondda to Pontypridd Living Memories
ISBN: 978-1-84589-560-0

British Library Cataloguing in Publication Data

Through the Rhondda to Pontypridd Living Memories
John A Milnes and Julia Skinner

The Francis Frith Collection
Unit 6, Oakley Business Park,
Wylye Road, Dinton,
Wiltshire SP3 5EU
Tel: +44 (0) 1722 716 376
Email: info@francisfrith.co.uk
www.francisfrith.com

Printed and bound in England

Front Cover: **TON PENTRE,** *Church Road c1965* T191001t
Frontispiece: **CWMPARC,** *Upper Cwmparc from Mountain Road c1960* C391008

The colour-tinting is for illustrative purposes only, and is not intended to be historically accurate

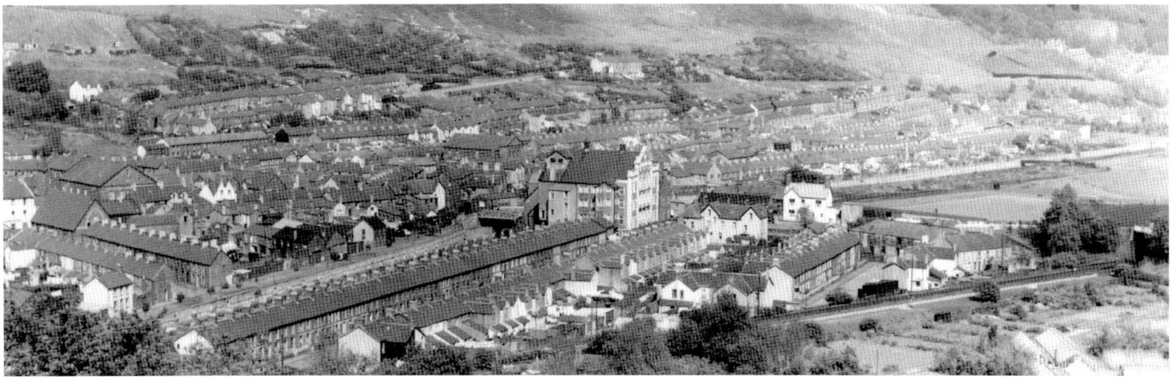

CONTENTS

FRANCIS FRITH
VICTORIAN PIONEER

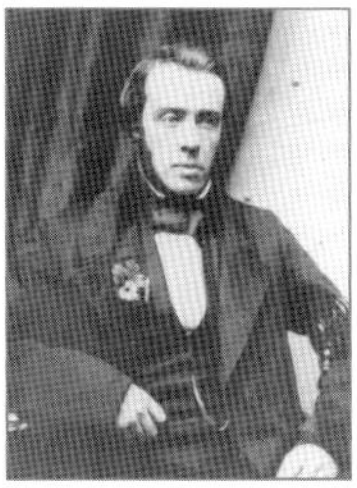

FRANCIS FRITH, founder of the world-famous photographic archive, was a complex and multi-talented man. A devout Quaker and a highly successful Victorian businessman, he was philosophic by nature and pioneering in outlook.

By 1855 he had already established a wholesale grocery business in Liverpool, and sold it for the astonishing sum of £200,000, which is the equivalent today of over £15,000,000. Now a very rich man, he was able to indulge his passion for travel. As a child he had pored over travel books written by early explorers, and his fancy and imagination had been stirred by family holidays to the sublime mountain regions of Wales and Scotland. 'What a land of spirit-stirring and enriching scenes and places!' he had written. He was to return to these scenes of grandeur in later years to 'recapture the thousands of vivid and tender memories', but with a different purpose. Now in his thirties, and captivated by the new science of photography, Frith set out on a series of pioneering journeys up the Nile and to the Near East that occupied him from 1856 until 1860.

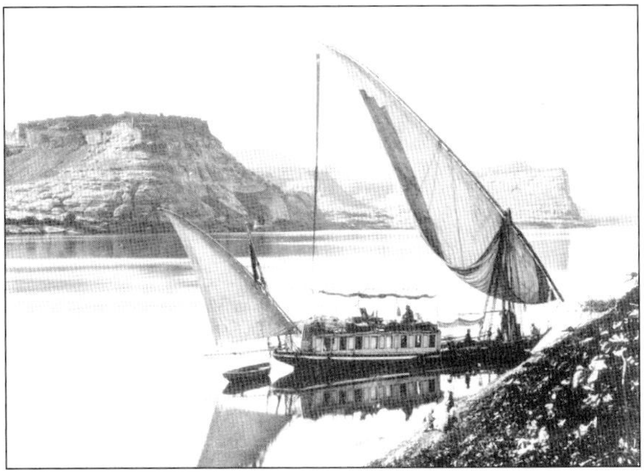

INTRIGUE AND EXPLORATION

These far-flung journeys were packed with intrigue and adventure. In his life story, written when he was sixty-three, Frith tells of being held captive by bandits, and of fighting 'an awful midnight battle to the very point of surrender with a deadly pack of hungry, wild dogs'. Wearing flowing Arab costume, Frith arrived at Akaba by camel sixty years before Lawrence of Arabia, where he encountered 'desert princes and rival sheikhs, blazing with jewel-hilted swords'.

He was the first photographer to venture beyond the sixth cataract of the Nile. Africa was still the mysterious 'Dark Continent', and Stanley and Livingstone's historic meeting was a decade into the future. The conditions for picture taking confound belief. He laboured for hours in his wicker dark-room in the sweltering heat of the desert, while the volatile chemicals fizzed dangerously in their trays. Back in London he exhibited his photographs and was 'rapturously cheered' by members of the Royal Society. His reputation as a photographer was made overnight.

VENTURE OF A LIFE-TIME

Characteristically, Frith quickly spotted the opportunity to create a new business as a specialist publisher of photographs. He lived in an era of immense and sometimes violent change. For the poor, in the early part of Victoria's reign, work was exhausting and the hours long, and people had precious little free time to enjoy themselves. Most people had no transport other than a cart or gig at their disposal, and rarely travelled far beyond the

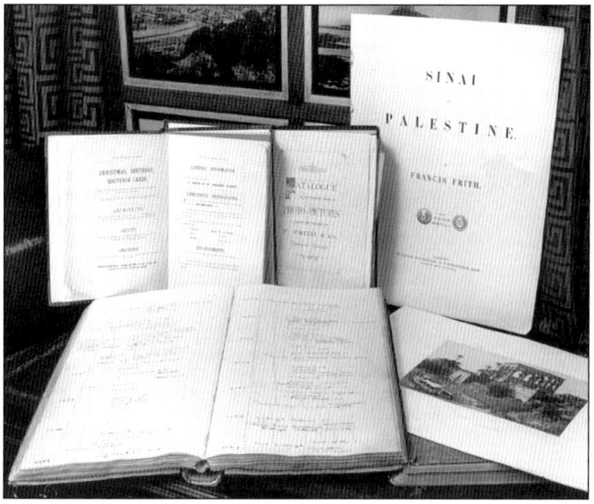

boundaries of their own town or village. However, by the 1870s the railways had threaded their way across the country, and Bank Holidays and half-day Saturdays had been made obligatory by Act of Parliament. All of a sudden the working man and his family were able to enjoy days out and see a little more of the world.

With typical business acumen, Francis Frith foresaw that these new tourists would enjoy having souvenirs to commemorate their days out. In 1860 he married Mary Ann Rosling and set out on a new career: his aim was to photograph every city, town and village in Britain. For the next thirty years he travelled the country by train and by pony and trap, producing fine photographs of seaside resorts and beauty spots that were keenly bought by millions of Victorians. These prints were painstakingly pasted into family albums and pored over during the dark nights of winter, rekindling precious memories of summer excursions.

THE RISE OF FRITH & CO

Frith's studio was soon supplying retail shops all over the country. To meet the demand he gathered about him a small team of photographers, and published the work of independent artist-photographers of the calibre of Roger Fenton and Francis Bedford. In order to gain some understanding of the scale of Frith's business one only has to look at the catalogue issued by Frith & Co in 1886: it runs to some 670 pages, listing not only many thousands of views of the British Isles but also many photographs of most European countries, and China, Japan, the USA and Canada - note the sample page shown on page 9 from the hand-written Frith & Co ledgers recording the pictures. By 1890 Frith had created the greatest specialist photographic publishing company in the world, with over 2,000 sales outlets - more than the combined number that Boots and WH Smith have today! The picture on the next page shows the Frith & Co display board at Ingleton in the Yorkshire Dales (left of window). Beautifully constructed with a mahogany frame and gilt inserts, it could display up to a dozen local scenes.

POSTCARD BONANZA

The ever-popular holiday postcard we know today took many years to develop. In 1870 the Post Office issued the first plain cards, with a pre-printed stamp on one face. In 1894 they allowed other publishers' cards to be sent through the mail with an attached adhesive halfpenny stamp. Demand grew rapidly, and in 1895 a new size of postcard was permitted called the court card, but there was little room for illustration. In 1899, a year after Frith's death, a new card measuring 5.5 x 3.5 inches became the standard format, but it was not until 1902 that the divided back came into being, so that the address and message could be on one face and a full-size illustration on the other. Frith & Co were in the vanguard of postcard development: Frith's sons Eustace and Cyril continued their father's monumental task, expanding the number of views offered to the public and recording more and more places in Britain, as the coasts and countryside were opened up to mass travel.

Francis Frith had died in 1898 at his villa in Cannes, his great project still growing. The archive he created continued in business for another seventy years. By 1970 it contained over a third of a million pictures showing 7,000 British towns and villages.

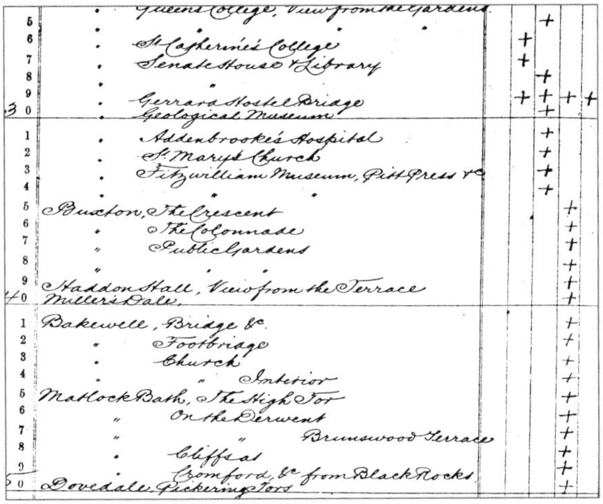

Queens College, View from the Gardens
5
6 St Catherine's College
7 Senate House & Library
8
9 Gerrard Hostel Bridge
30 Geological Museum
1 Addenbrooke's Hospital
2 St Mary's Church
3 Fitzwilliam Museum, Pitt Press &c
4
5 Buxton, The Crescent
6 " The Colonnade
7 " Public Gardens
8
9 Haddon Hall, View from the Terrace
40 Miller's Dale.
1 Bakewell, Bridge &c.
2 " Footbridge
3 " Church
4 " " Interior
5 Matlock Bath, The High Tor
6 " On the Derwent
7 " " Brunswood Terrace
8 " Cliffs at
9 Cromford, &c from Black Rocks
50 Dovedale, Pickering Tors

FRANCIS FRITH'S LEGACY

Frith's legacy to us today is of immense significance and value, for the magnificent archive of evocative photographs he created provides a unique record of change in the cities, towns and villages throughout Britain over a century and more. Frith and his fellow studio photographers revisited locations many times down the years to update their views, compiling for us an enthralling and colourful pageant of British life and character.

We are fortunate that Frith was dedicated to recording the minutiae of everyday life. For it is this sheer wealth of visual data, the painstaking chronicle of changes in dress, transport, street layouts, buildings, housing, engineering and landscape that captivates us so much today. His remarkable images offer us a powerful link with the past and with the lives of our ancestors.

THE VALUE OF THE ARCHIVE TODAY

Computers have now made it possible for Frith's many thousands of images to be accessed almost instantly. Frith's images are increasingly used as visual resources, by social historians, by researchers into genealogy and ancestry, by architects and town planners, and by teachers involved in local history projects.

In addition, the archive offers every one of us an opportunity to examine the places where we and our families have lived and worked down the years. Highly successful in Frith's own era, the archive is now, a century and more on, entering a new phase of popularity. Historians consider the Francis Frith Collection to be of prime national importance. It is the only archive of its kind remaining in private ownership. Francis Frith's archive is now housed in an historic timber barn in the beautiful village of Teffont in Wiltshire. Its founder would not recognize the archive office as it is today. In place of the many thousands of dusty boxes containing glass plate negatives and an all-pervading odour of photographic chemicals, there are now ranks of computer screens. He would be amazed to watch his images travelling round the world at unimaginable speeds through internet lines.

The archive's future is both bright and exciting. Francis Frith, with his unshakeable belief in making photographs available to the greatest number of people, would undoubtedly approve of what is being done today with his lifetime's work. His photographs depicting our shared past are now bringing pleasure and enlightenment to millions around the world a century and more after his death.

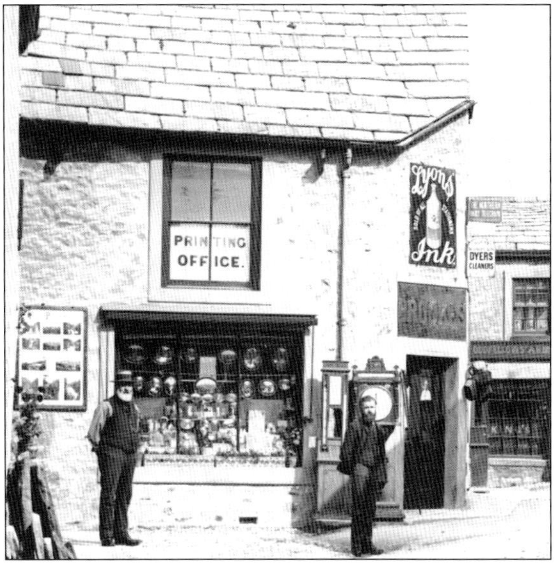

THE RHONDDA
AN INTRODUCTION

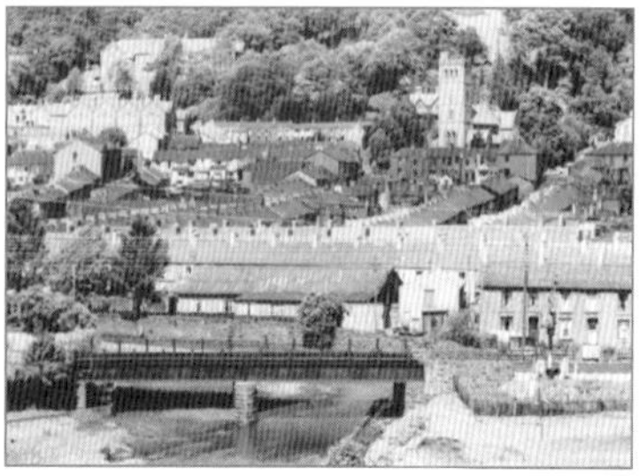

OF ALL THE PLACE NAMES in Wales, the Rhondda is probably the best known, perhaps with the exception of Snowdonia. One thing is certain, though: the name itself is one of the most evocative of all. To most people it signifies just two things, coal and male voice choirs. There is much, much more to the Rhondda, but no one would dispute that coal made the Rhondda and that the miners made the choirs.

Wales is fiercely protective of its reputation as a land of song, and the voice of Wales is most commonly heard amongst the ranks of male voice choirs. Although they can be found all over the country, it is in the southern industrial heartland that they seem to be loudest and strongest. The roots of the choirs lie in the Nonconformist religious traditions of the 17th and 18th centuries, when Methodism

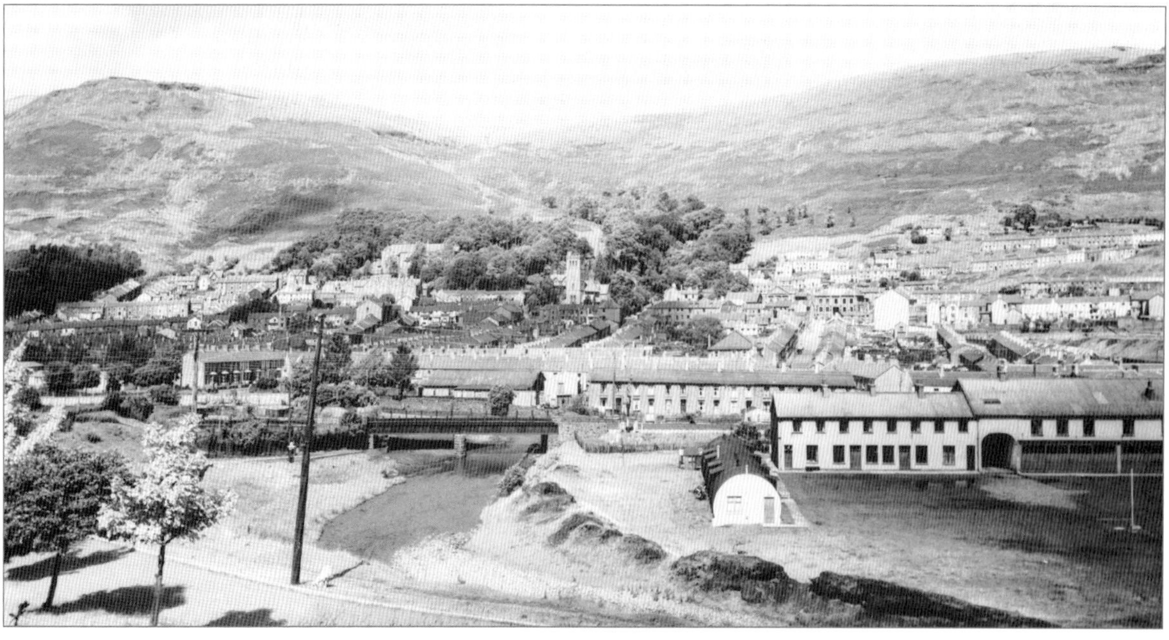

PENTRE, *General View c1965* P225006

in particular swept the country and singing was a free and potent way of cherishing the frequently persecuted faith. Throughout the swift industrialisation of the 19th century in the Glamorgan valleys, choirs of miners came together to praise God in the fervently religious way that was typical of the crowded and poor communities. Classic hymns like 'Cwm Rhondda' and the Welsh national anthem 'Mae Hen Wlad Fy Nhadau' ('Land of my Fathers') are synonymous with the choirs, whose full-bodied interpretation of them makes all other efforts seem third-rate and insipid. The collapse of mining in the 20th century left many choirs perilously short of members, but most continue to practise with strict devotion.

The Rhondda is a small region around two river valleys in mid-Glamorgan, each about sixteen miles long and never as much as a mile wide. The twin valleys lie approximately fifteen miles north of Cardiff, the Welsh capital. The Rhondda Fawr river (Big Rhondda) runs for ten miles, while the Rhondda Fach (Small Rhondda) is seven miles long. The two valleys form a V shape, and come together in the south of the Rhondda at the confluence of the two rivers in the appropriately named town of Porth, meaning 'gateway'. The two valleys are separated by the Cefn-y-Rhondda ridge, which reaches nearly 1,700 feet, and Mynydd Maerdy.

So, a logical tour of the area would be to start to the north of the Rhondda Fawr at Treherbert and journey south through Treorchy, then, after a diversion to Cwmparc, to Ton Pentre and Ystrad. Continuing southwards in the pages of this book, we go through Llwynypia, Tonypandy, Trealaw and Penygraig before arriving in Porth; then the trip swings north up the valley of the Rhondda Fach through Ynyshir and Ferndale. Finally, we visit Pontypridd, where the converged Rhondda Fawr and Rhondda Fach empty into the Taff.

Thus it is clear that the region we know as the Rhondda is a tiny area. Having said that, the Rhondda certainly had a part to play in the development of Wales and the economy of the UK. It was the heart of the South Wales coal industry, an industry that in the past provided around one third of the entire world output of coal. The Rhondda was particularly renowned for the high-grade bituminous and steam coals which were found here. The region's quintessential heritage was typified by struggling hillside communities. Hollywood played its part in promoting the area, perhaps a little too sentimentally for some tastes, in the 1941 Oscar-winning film 'How Green Was My Valley'. Richard Llewellyn, the author of the novel on which the film was based, stayed briefly in Gilfach Goch to collect background material for his story. Although Gilfach Goch is not actually in the Rhondda, the story of 'How Green Was My Valley' is typical of the whole region and a vivid recounting of a childhood spent in the lush hills of Wales. A coal-mining family experiences labour unrest and personal tragedy as their traditional way of life collides with the 20th century. The story has an even greater poignancy for the valley people, because the only person to benefit directly and financially was the author. It is one of Hollywood's best-kept secrets that the movie was not filmed in Wales. Owing to the inherent dangers of the Second World War, an 80-acre studio-built set was constructed in the Santa Monica hills to create a make-believe Wales. If that was not enough, the picture had to be shot in black and white, as the sun-baked California setting was far from green!

Back in 1860, when the Rhondda was described as 'wild and untameable', there were no roads into the valleys, and indeed why should there have been? It was simply a densely forested area, which abounded with game and wildlife. It was said that a squirrel could travel tree by tree from the rivers' sources at the heads of the valleys all the way down to Pontypridd without touching the ground.

All this was to change – and rapidly. In the mid-19th century, tentative mining explorations had taken place in the quiet, lush valleys, and black gold was struck – vast deposits of bituminous and steam coal – the Lower Coal Series – were found. These coals had a high carbon and calorific content and were particularly in demand, especially by the Royal Navy. In 1855 the first consignment of Rhondda coal was sent to Cardiff. At that time, the two valleys housed around 3,000 people. By 1910, nearly 160,000 were squeezed into the available land, in ranks and terraces of houses grouped around 60 or so pitheads. Take Treherbert, for example: in the early 19th century, Treherbert was an untouched idyll. A tourist of the time described at as 'a truly picturesque district which has been called the Alps of Glamorgan'. Later, the Reverend D A Lewis was to point out that coal mining had become the mainstay of a town like this. 'The life of our Parish depends entirely on the production of coal. All its activities are in gear with the labourers who work on the coal face. Behind the colliers are the hauliers, the repairers, the maintenance workers, and on the outside are the transport workers'. In 1801 the population of Treherbert was 542, and by 1871 it was 16,914. These figures speak for themselves.

Mining the Rhondda coal was one thing, but the Marquess of Bute knew that the key to the success of the coal industry lay in getting the coal out of the Rhondda to the ports of Cardiff and Barry, and so he gained control of the canals, railways and roads. His fortune made him the richest man in Britain – he was a billionaire by today's terms – and his legacy to Wales was that in virtually every South Wales town there is a Bute Street. Massive fortunes were made by the few on the sweating backs of the many who toiled in the Rhondda coal mines. Shafts of unprecedented depth were sunk, and down them the miners were sent to work in appalling and dangerous conditions. The worst disaster in the history of British coalmining occurred in 1913 at Senghenydd in the Aber valley east of Pontypridd, when 439 people died after being trapped underground by an explosion and fire which spread through the tunnels of the mine, but the Rhondda had its own stories of tragedy: 114 died after an explosion at Cymmer Colliery near Porth in 1856; 178 were killed at Ferndale in 1867; 96 died in a disaster at Naval Colliery, Tonypandy, in 1880; 81 were killed on Christmas Eve 1885 at Maerdy; 57 died at Tylorstown in 1896, and 119 at the National Colliery, Wattstown in 1905, to chronicle just a few. Aside from these disasters, many other people working in the coalmining industry suffered occupation-related health problems which contributed to an early death or disability.

The Rhondda became a self-reliant, chapel-going, deeply poor and terrifically spirited community, and a breeding ground for radical religion and firebrand politics. The Communist Party, which could hardly gain a foothold in England, ran the town of Maerdy for decades – Maerdy, at the head of the Rhondda Fach valley, was nicknamed 'Little Moscow' by Fleet Street in the 1930s. Sadly, there are no photographs of Maerdy in The Francis Frith Collection to include in this book, but it holds an important place in the history of the Rhondda – it was the home of the last deep mine in the region.

By the 1980s it was all but over for the Welsh coal industry. Though far from exhausted, the Rhondda deep mine pits were considered uneconomic when compared with the environmentally destructive method of open cast mining. Open cast mining was cheaper, but it blitzed vast areas of land and cost thousands of jobs, not only in Wales but also across the country. The 1984/85 miners' strike saw a quality of solidarity in South Wales unequalled in any other part of the land. But the Tory government was not listening, let alone talking, and the final pit in the Rhondda closed four days before Christmas 1990. True, there were reasonably generous redundancy payments (many saw these as bribes); but these were no compensation for the generations of proud working men, whose only request was to work.

It is often assumed by people outside the area that the all but absolute death of the coal industries has left the landscape irreparably scarred. In fact, the opposite has happened; the Rhondda is now an area undergoing a remarkable regeneration, populated with friendly and forward-looking people. The beauty of the landscape has returned, and the mountains are again green; there are no more coal tips and slag heaps, whose great peaks once stood like the pyramids of old, reaching up to

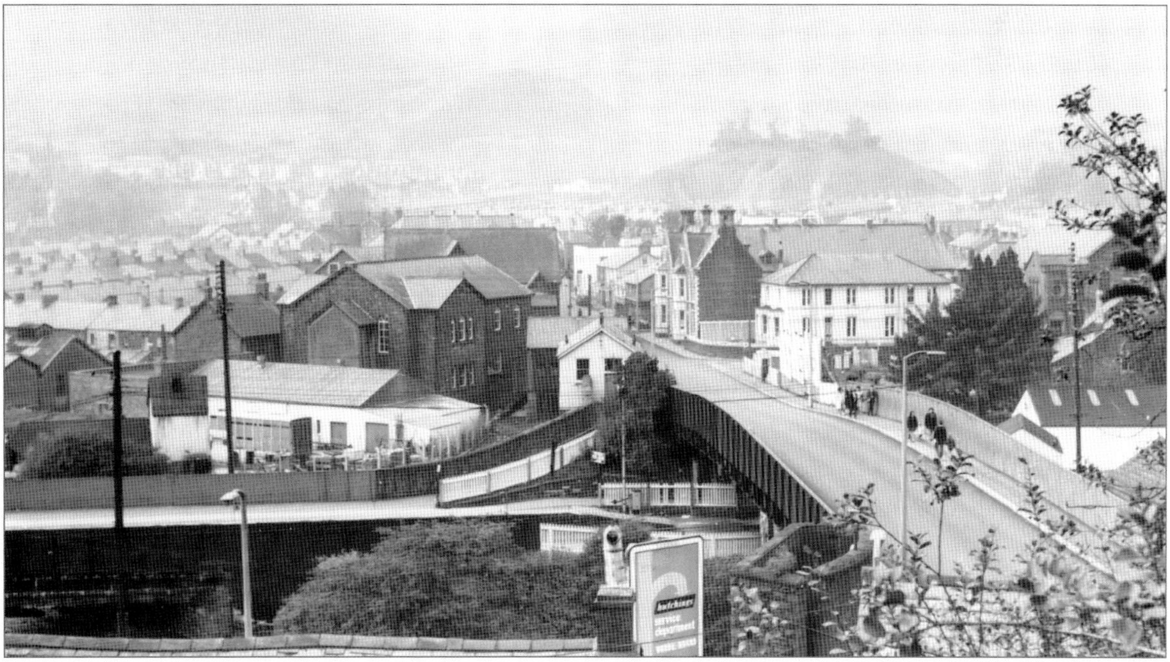

TON PENTRE *c1960* T191019

the sky. The mine shafts have been capped and the colliery buildings demolished. The areas where they once stood have been redeveloped, and the descendants of coal miners now make their livings in other ways.

As we walk along the top of mountains, we can look down into the valleys where terraced houses are perched, and where the roads, rivers and railways snake together through the tight curves of the hills. We can see for miles over the green valleys; it is a different world from the hustle and bustle of the big cities. As an old miner once said, "When you walk along the mountain tops of the Rhondda, you are closer to God, and so you don't have so far to travel when He calls".

What lies in the future for the Rhondda? The continuing development of the commercial centres here, together with constant improvements to communications, makes the area attractive to new developments. The valleys' retail and service sectors continue to improve, expand and diversify to complement the advances of the industrial/manufacturing base, and commerce is thriving. The constant improvement of the environment of the Rhondda is being achieved through the Council's programme of land reclamation; this continues to transform the area, making it extremely attractive to housing developers. Major improvements have also been made to the roads, both those inside the Rhondda and

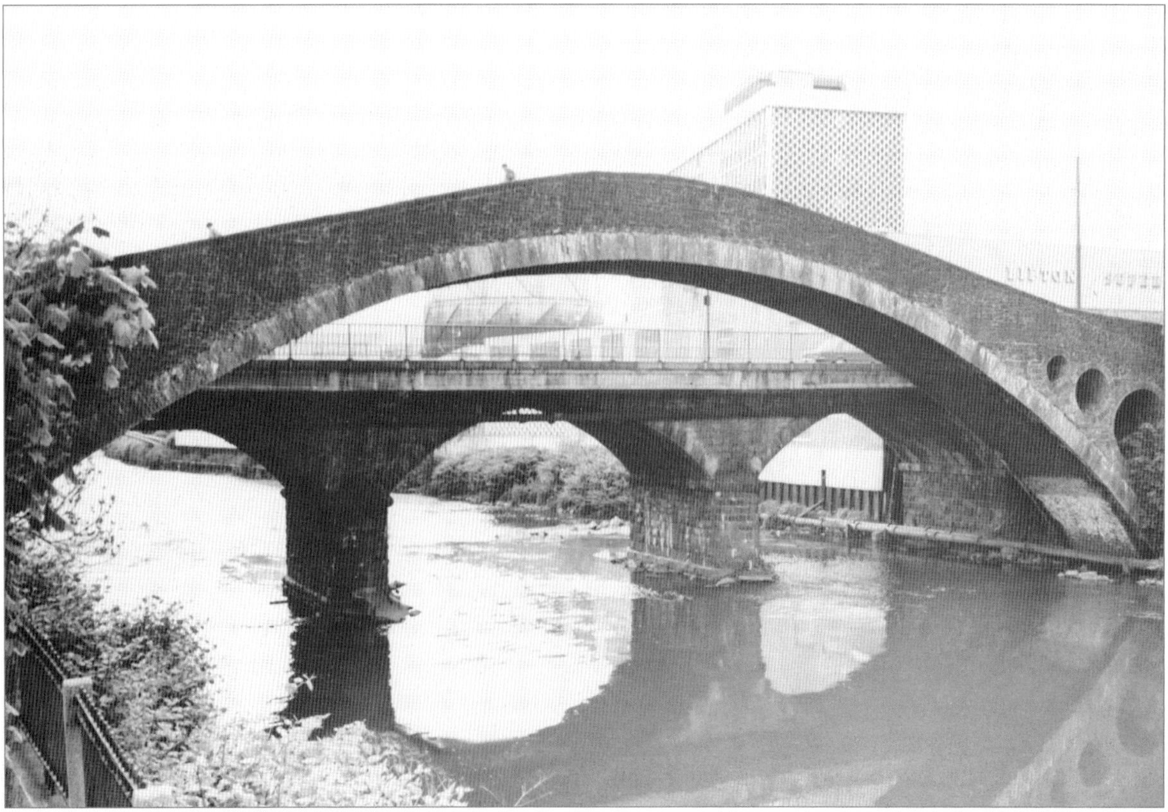

PONTYPRIDD, *The Old Bridge c1960* P716041

those connecting the valleys to the surrounding major road networks. More by-passes and relief roads are planned. Consideration is being given to the provision of heliport facilities within the Rhondda to carer for the ever-increasing demands that will be placed upon the business community, their suppliers and their customers as business continues to grow in the region. The Council's positive strategy to continue the development of recreation and tourism will ensure the further imaginative improvement of both inside and outside facilities, as well as the enhancement of the arts and cultural heritage in general. The industrial heritage of the area is celebrated in the Rhondda Heritage Park Visitor Centre, which opened in 1989 in the stores building of the old Lewis Merthyr Colliery at Trehafod. The story of coalmining which is told there, and of the people of the Rhondda who worked in the industry, and their cultural and social heritage, has proved to be of interest to more than just local residents, attracting visitors to the centre from all over Britain.

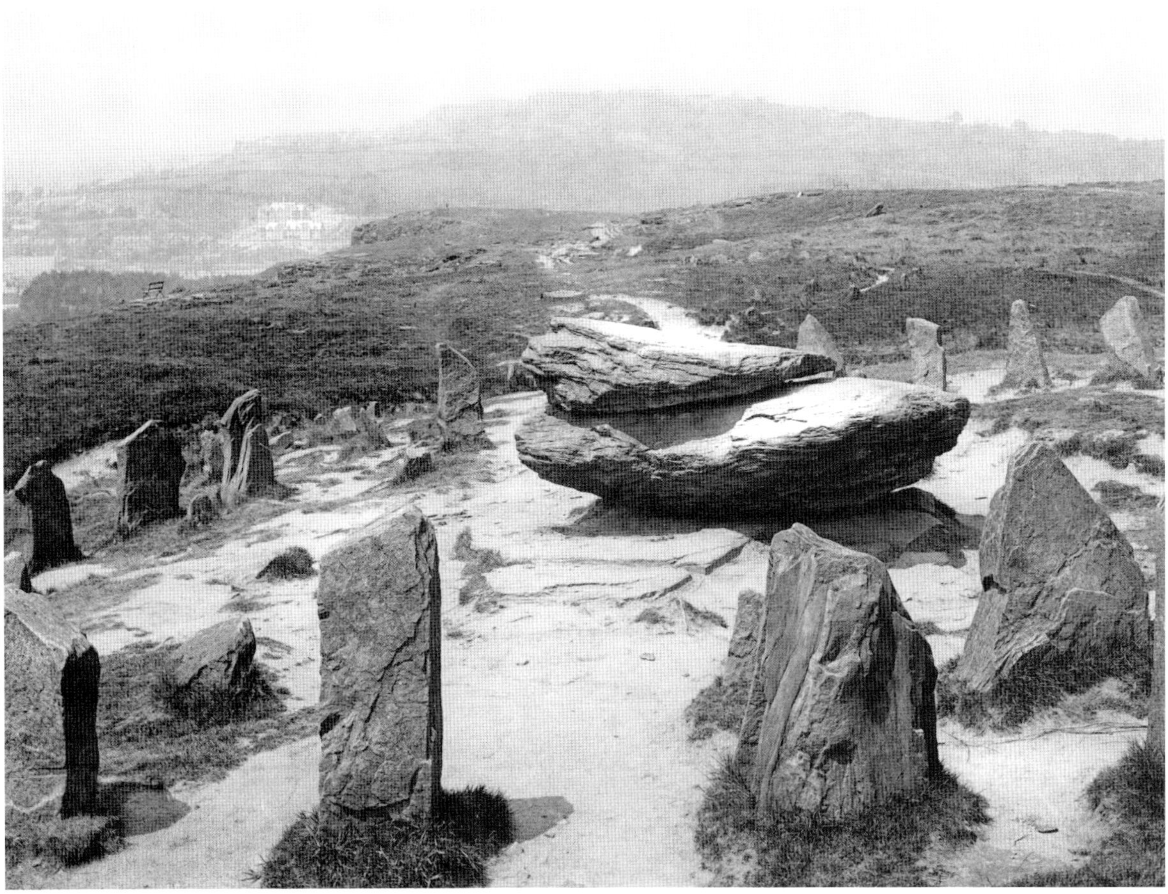

PONTYPRIDD, *The Rocking Stone 1899* 43620

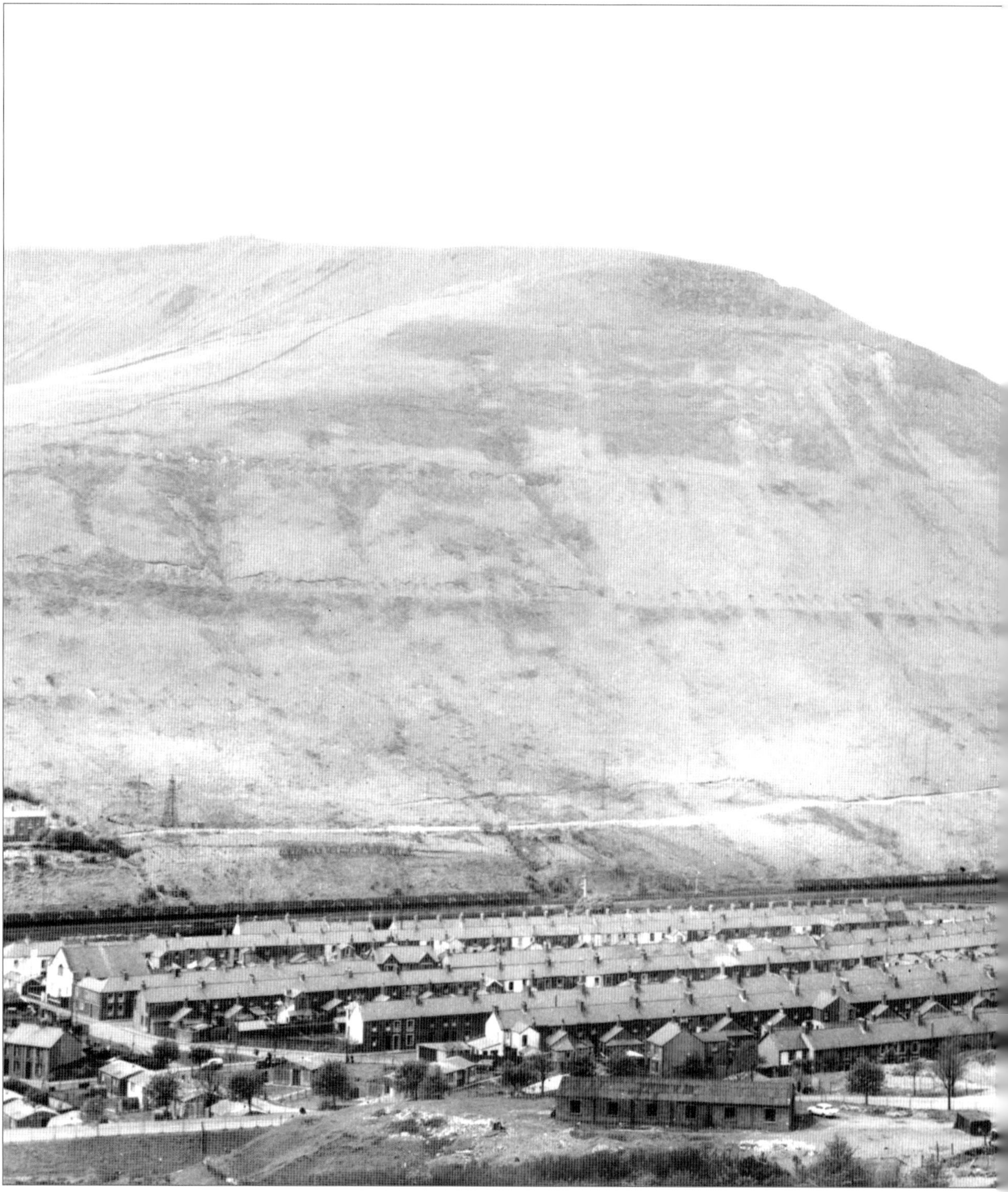

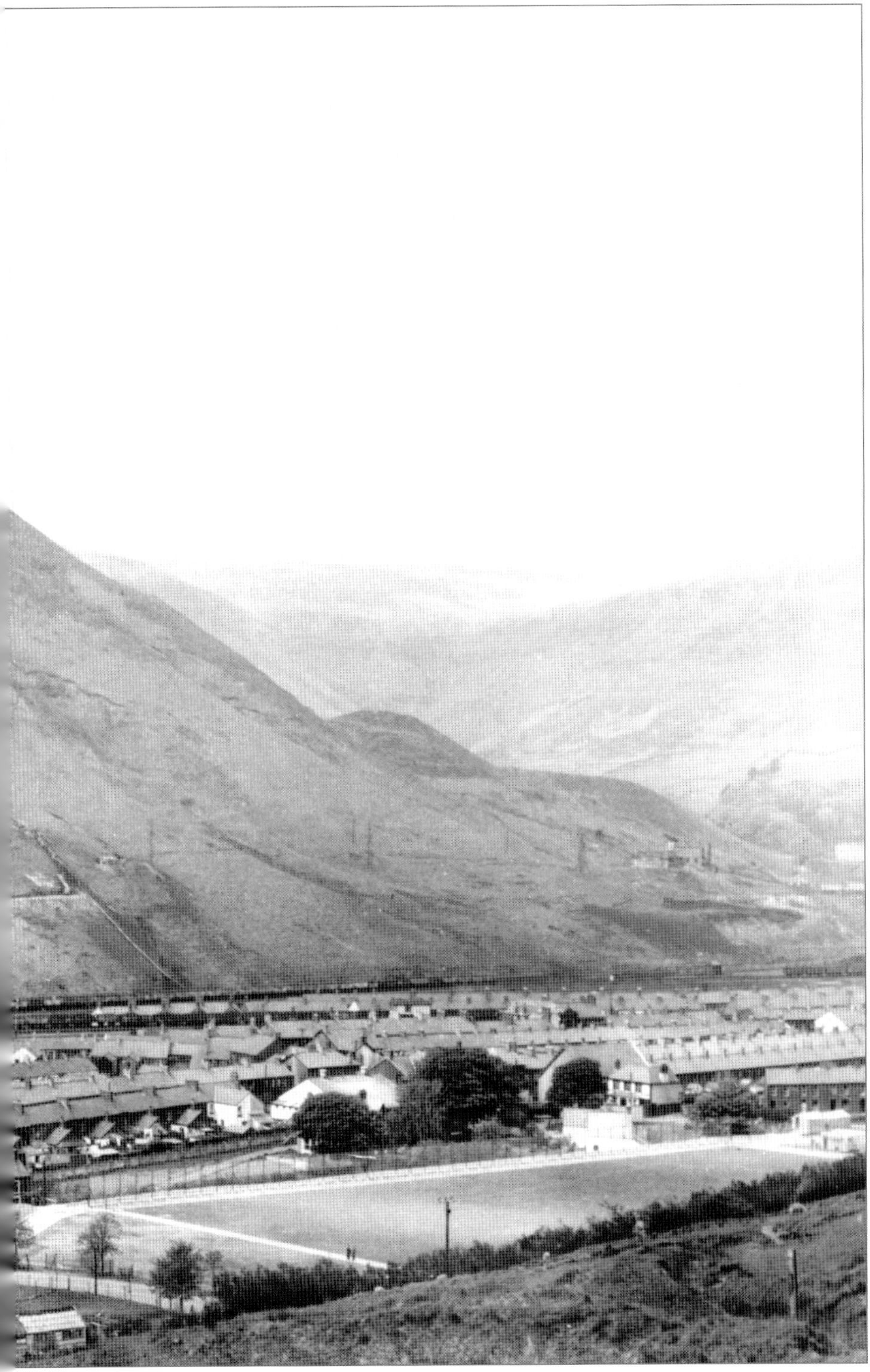

TYNEWYDD
Craig-y-Ddellw Mountain c1955 T198029

The picture clearly shows the perspective of the valley. The mountain towers over the valley floor, so narrow that the rows of terraces have no room to spread upward but are restricted to the narrowness of the valley floor.

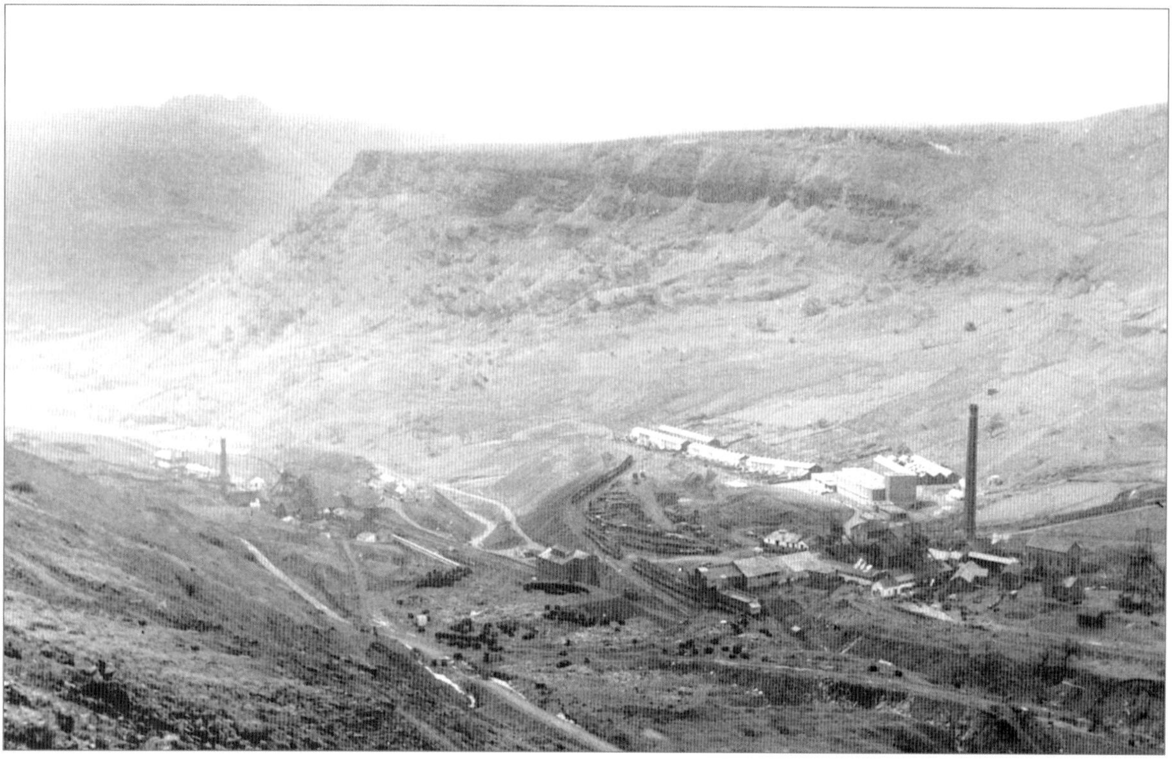

TREHERBERT, *The View from the New Road c1955* T196012

Below the barren and glaciated escarpment lies the Glenrhondda Colliery of Treherbert.

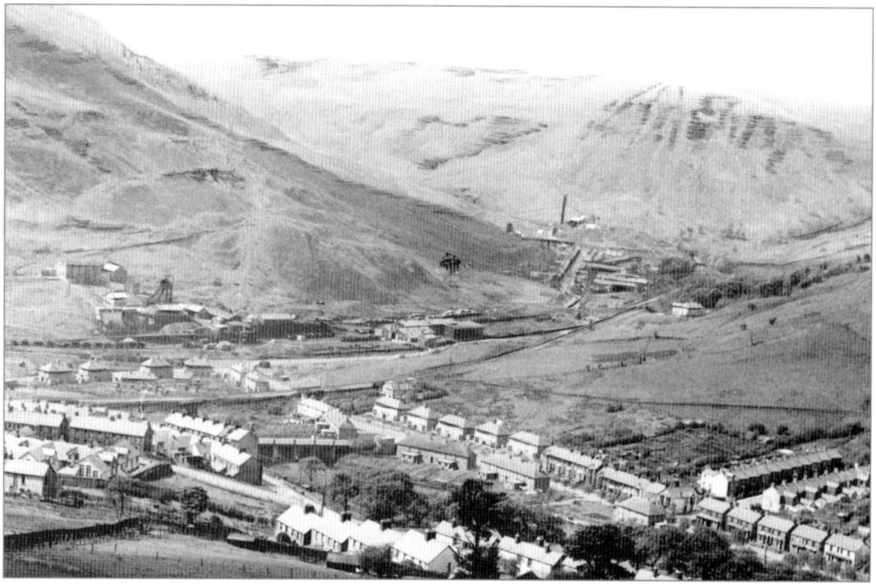

TREHERBERT
The View from the New Road c1960 T196013

A different angle shows the two pits with the winding house clearly visible at the left hand one. Beyond the collieries the hills are still scarred and blackened at the time of this photograph whereas on this side of the valley the cleaner air is allowing some tree growth.

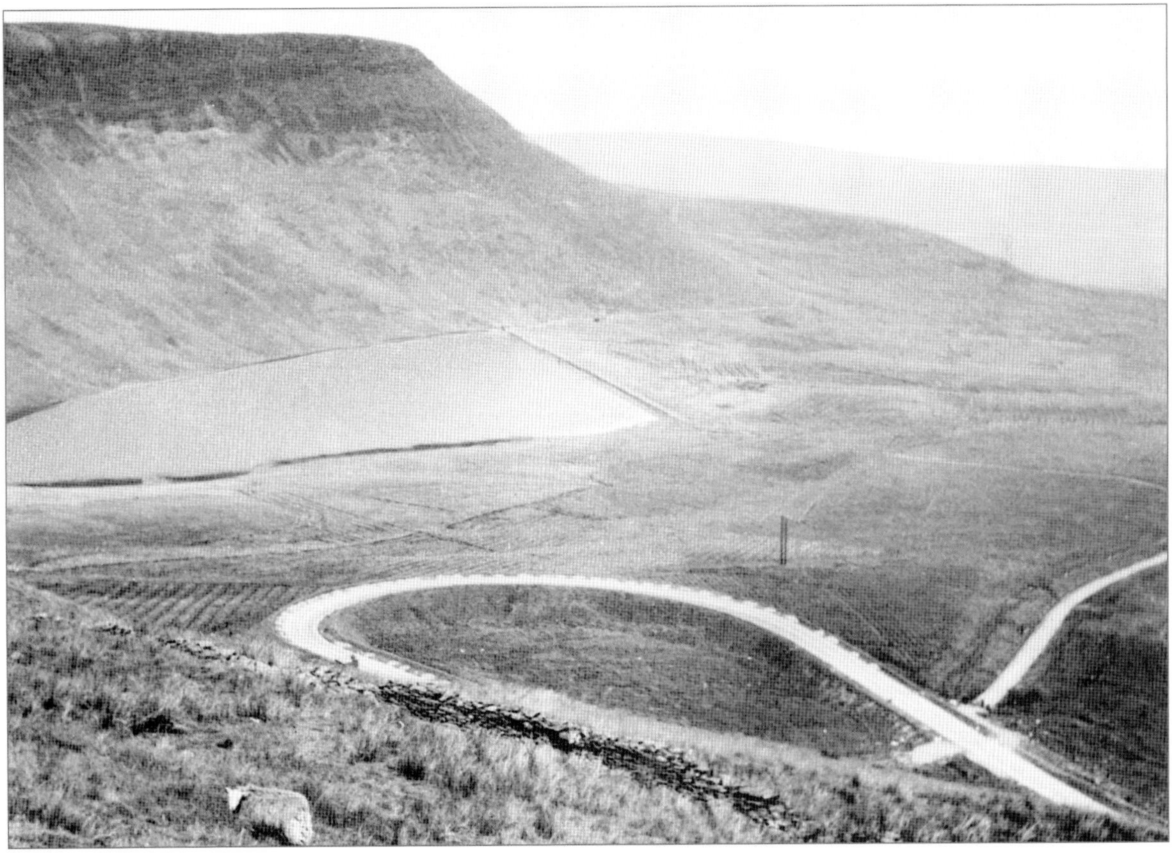

TREHERBERT

The Llyn and Horseshoe Bend c1960 T196019

This is a real gem of a picture for geologists and naturalists. The 'Llyn' is 'Llyn Fawr', one of the southernmost glaciated lakes in Britain, which lies at the foot of the sandstone escarpment of Craig-y-Llyn. The lake is now used as a reservoir. The area is designated of 'Special Scientific Interest' due to the presence of the rare Smooth and Palmate Newts. This spot is also home to kestrels and buzzards as well as the much rarer peregrines and sparrow hawks. And why should anyone build a road in such a fashion? Well, simply because the area of bog and quicksand around the 'Llyn' forced the road builders on to solid ground, and it would be impossible for a car to climb to the top of Craig-y-Llyn without a horseshoe bend. There is a second bend halfway up the mountain that brings you onto the top.

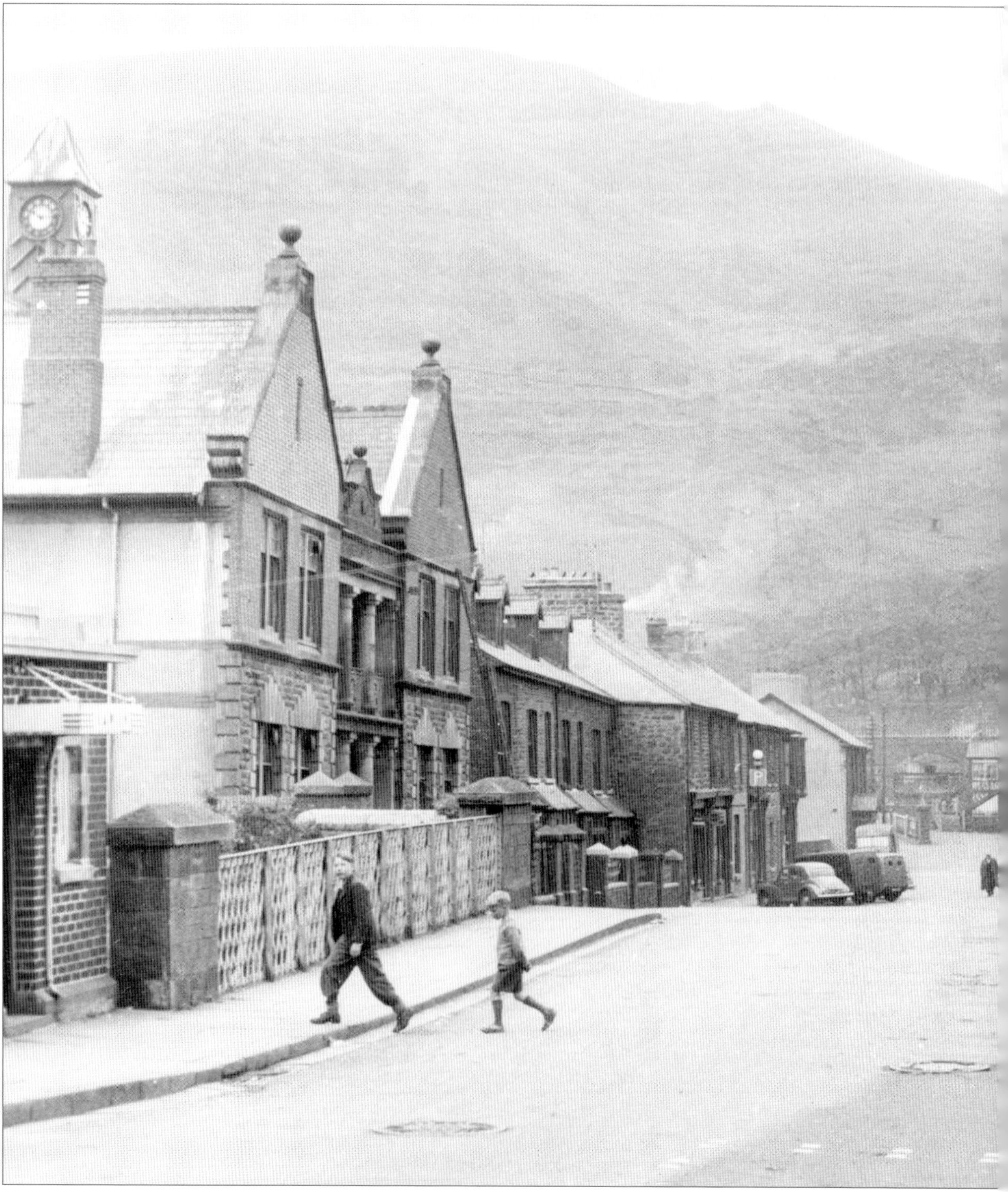

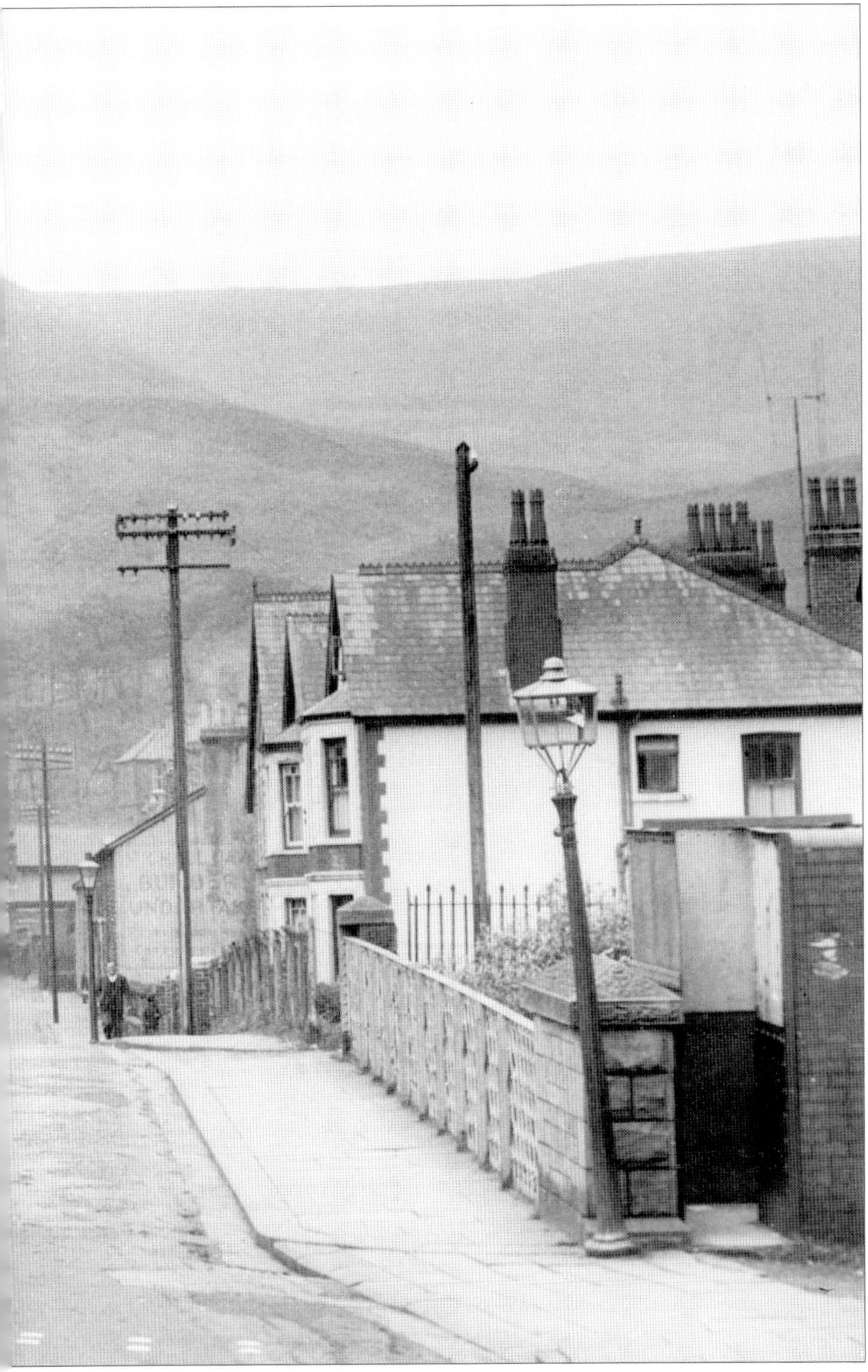

TREHERBERT
Station Road c1955
T196001

The road leading out of this village, climbing the north-eat flank of the head of the valley, was built in 1930-32 by unemployed miners.

TREHERBERT
Bute Street c1955 T196008

Like many places in South Wales, Bute Street in Treherbert is named after the 2nd Marquess of Bute, who was so important in the development of the Welsh coal industry. Wide and straight, there is one struggling tree on the left but a wonderful array of every type of shop across the road. As far as the eye can see this bay-windowed terrace contains such names as 'Dawes and Sons', 'J E Jones', 'Havard and Son', whatever their trade. No doubting that 'Peglers' is the grocer with his window advertising 'English Bacon' and 'Butter at 2/6d'.

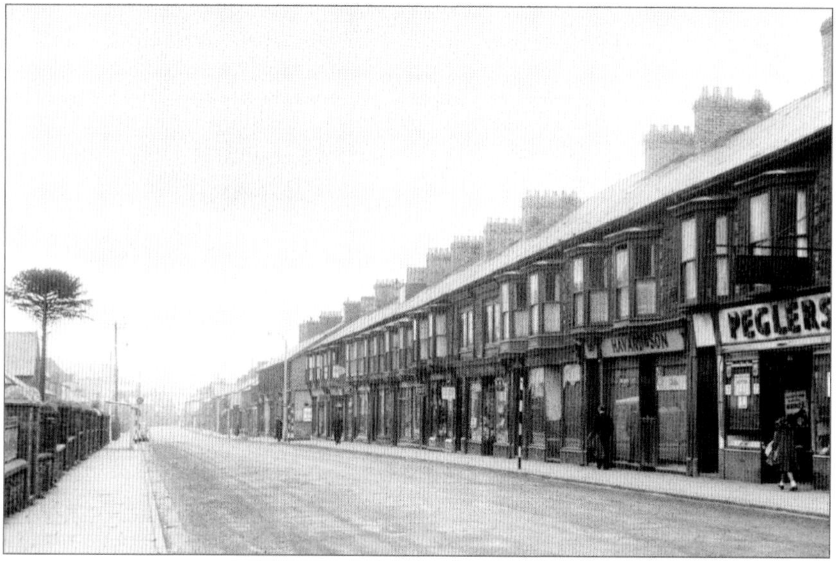

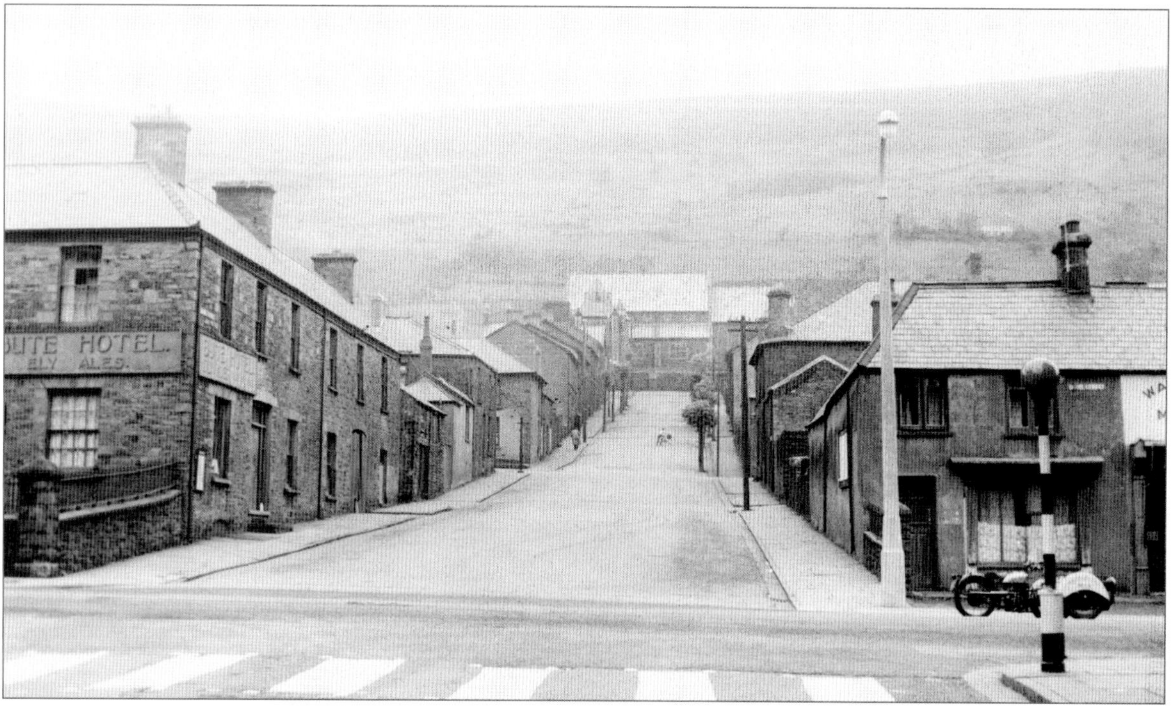

TREHERBERT, *Church Street c1955* T196004

The nicely composed photo takes the eye-line along the street towards the church, crossing the ubiquitous 'Bute Street' on its way. The 'Bute Hotel' not only sold Ely ales but had a back room used by the Nonconformists for prayer meetings. On the right, across from the 'Belisha' beacon is a motorbike and sidecar - a common sight in the valleys, used by businesses for deliveries - with the slogan 'Pasteurised Milk' on the rear mudguard.

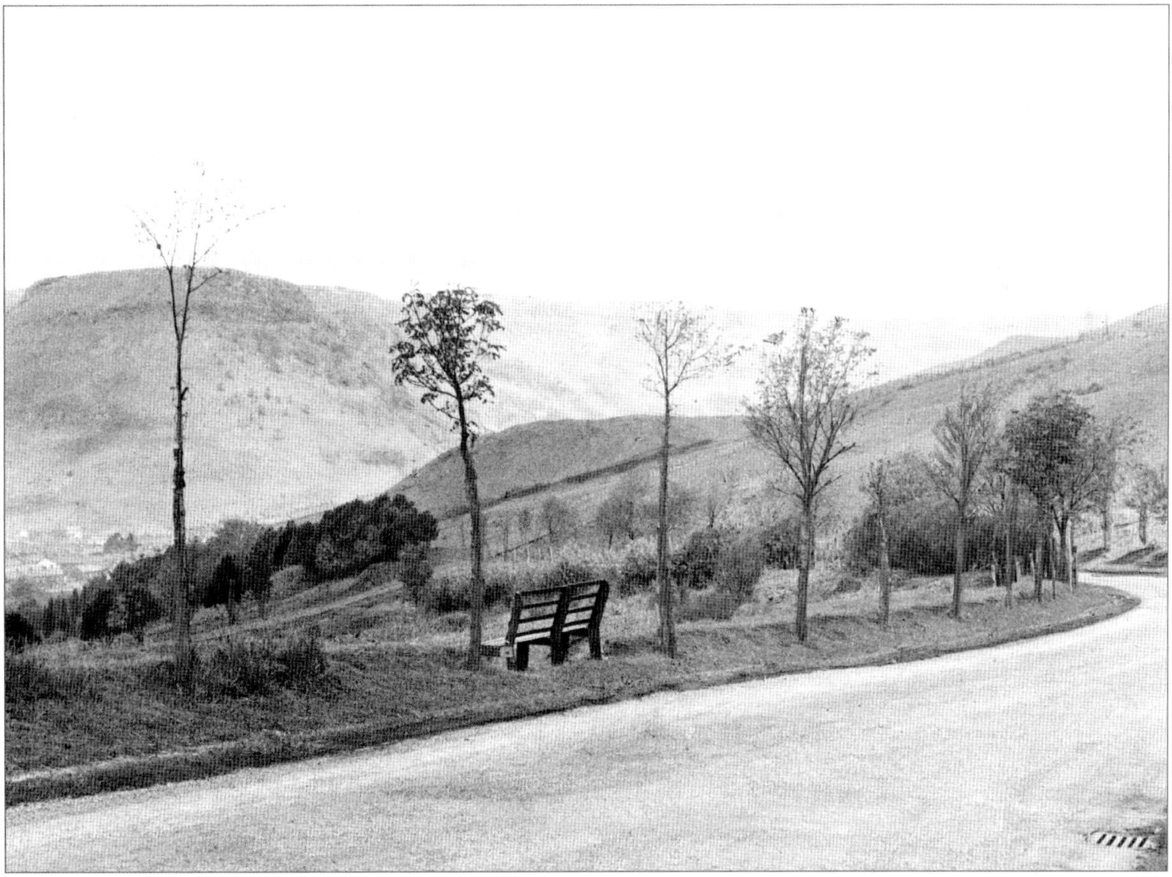

TREHERBERT
New Road c1960 T196015

The original name of Treherbert was Cwm-Saebren, and the first steam-coal pit in the Rhondda was sunk here in 1855, after the trustees of the Marquess of Bute bought Cwm-Saebren Farm. Treherbert was one of the family names of the Marquess of Bute, and is first recorded in 1855.

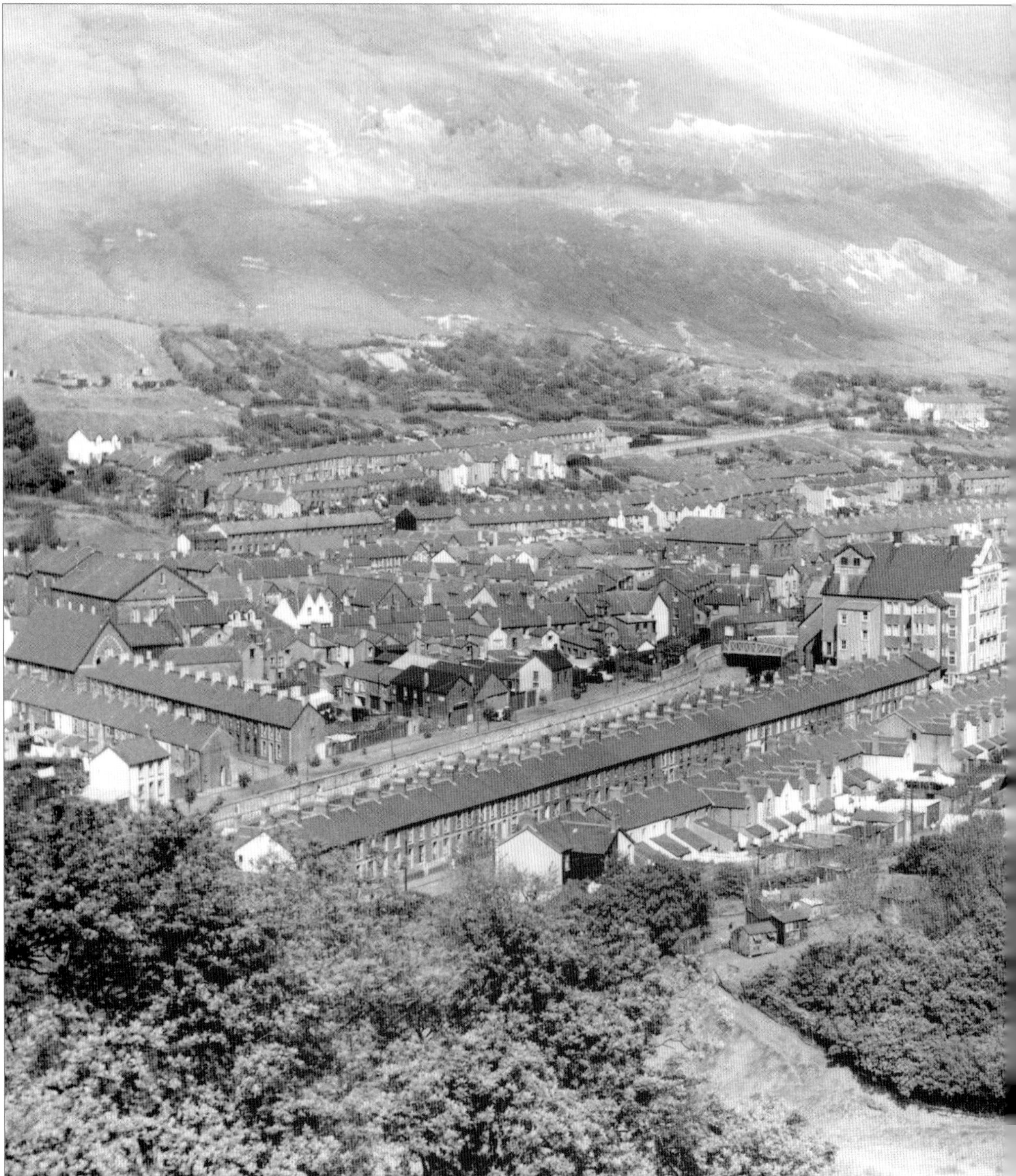

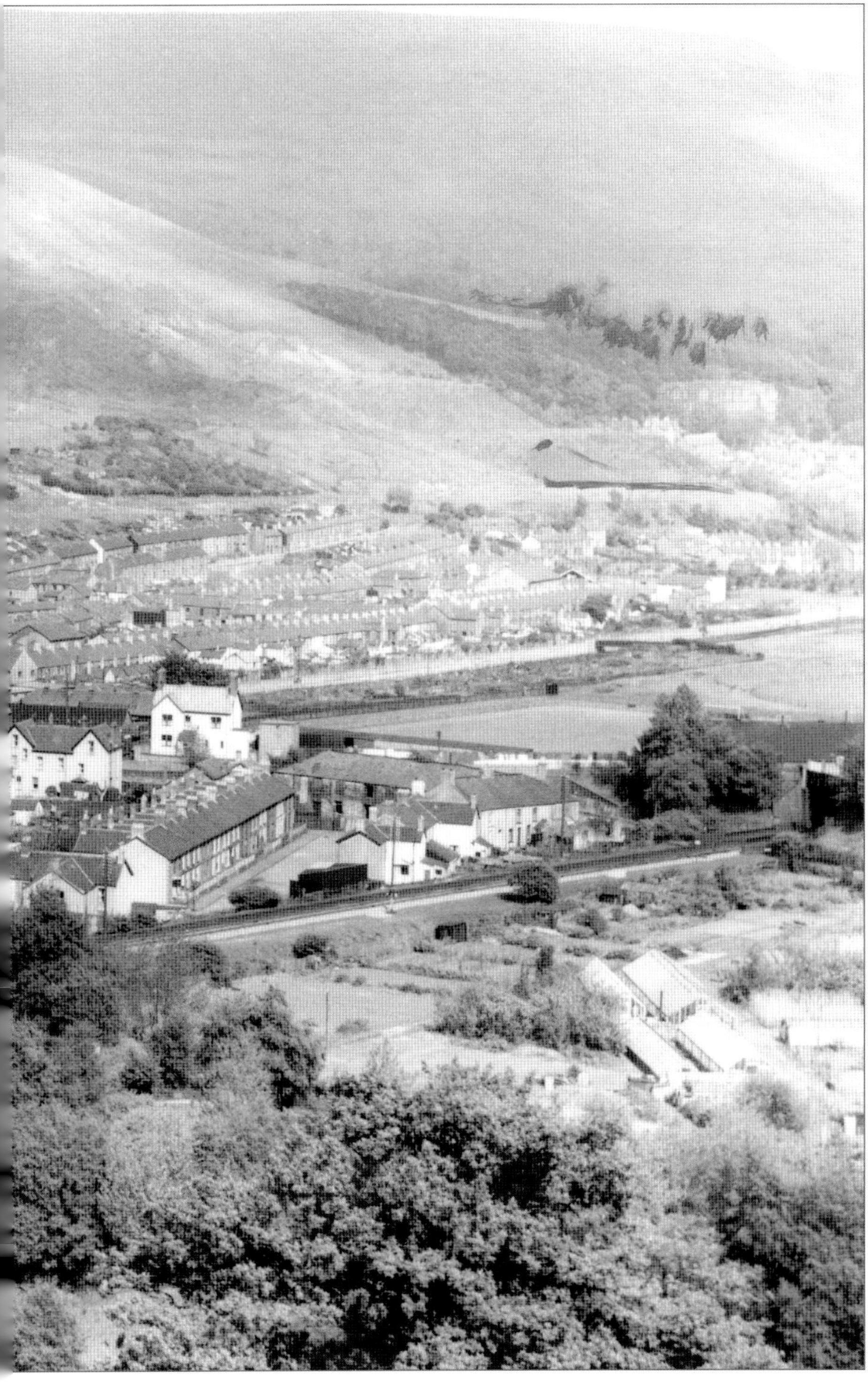

TREORCHY
General View c1960
T197053
Often spelled 'Treorci', this village is only a mile or so south of Treherbert. The grand building in the centre of this photograph is four storeys high and is the 'Parc and Dare Theatre', a beautifully restored mock-Georgian edifice. It is so grand it is almost out of place in the Rhondda, not known for superb architecture. The 'Parc and Dare' makes up for a general lack and would match any city in Europe for its magnificence.
It should be said the Treorchy was not just another mining settlement. It is one of the most famous places in Wales due to the international status of its Royal Male Voice Choir, the oldest in the country.

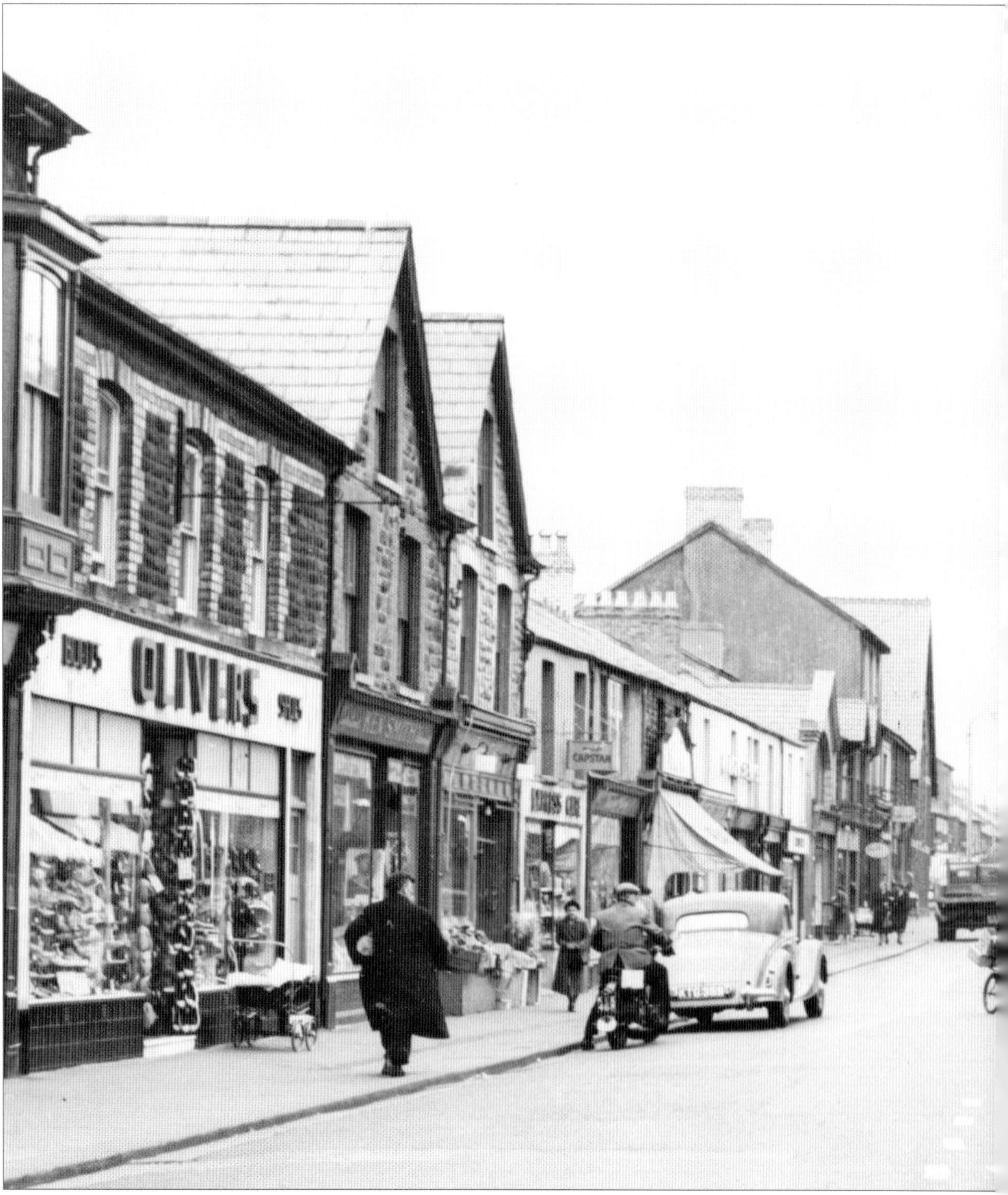
OLIVER'S
CAPSTAN

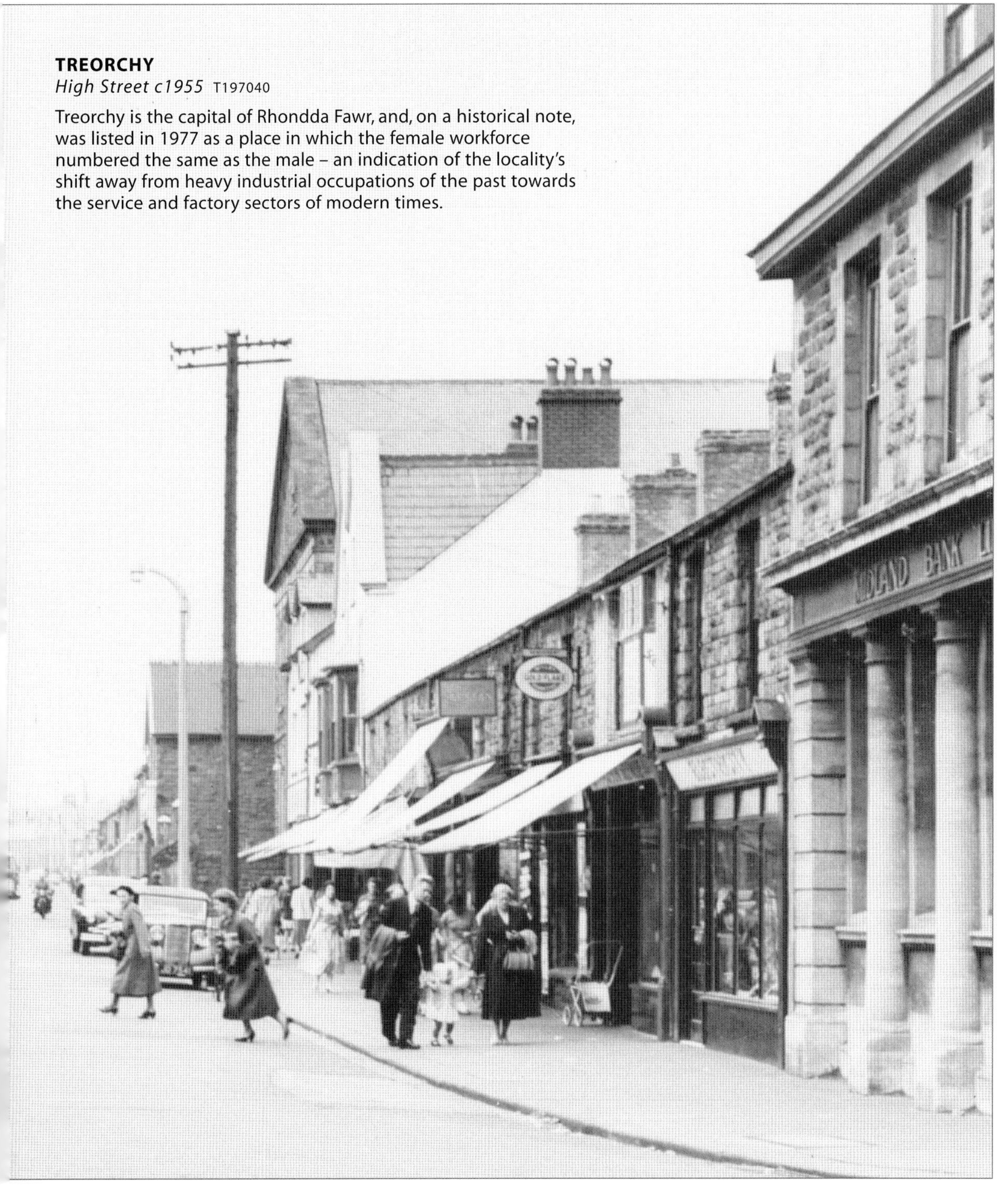

TREORCHY
High Street c1955 T197040

Treorchy is the capital of Rhondda Fawr, and, on a historical note, was listed in 1977 as a place in which the female workforce numbered the same as the male – an indication of the locality's shift away from heavy industrial occupations of the past towards the service and factory sectors of modern times.

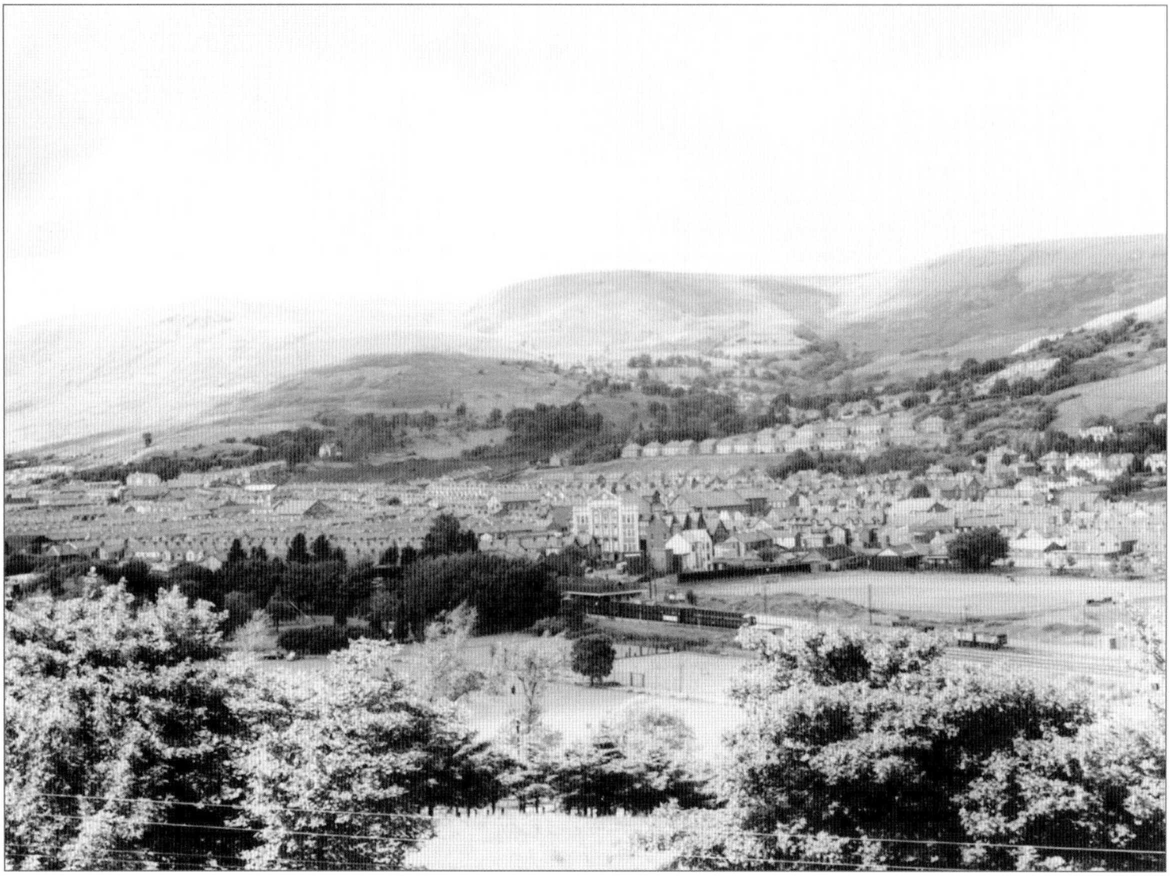

TREORCHY

General View c1965 T197075

Carriages and trucks of the Taff Railway can be seen in this photograph. The 'Parc and Dare' is prominent in the centre of this view.

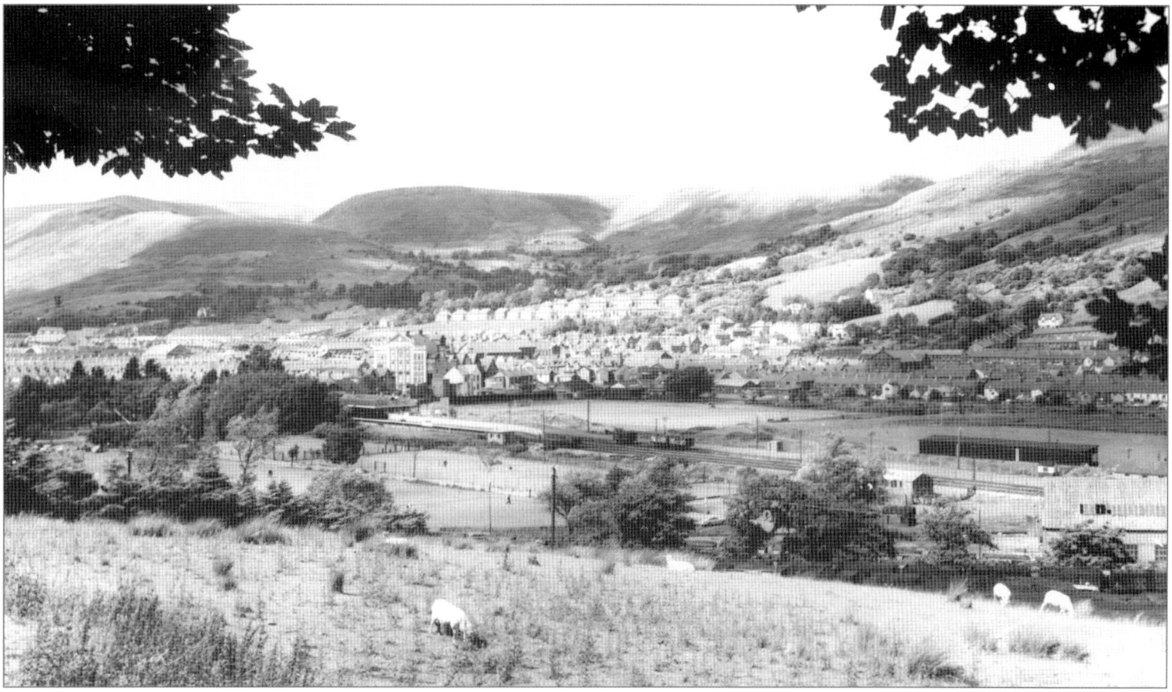

▲ **TREORCHY,** *General View c1960* T197076

The railway is in clear view in this photograph.

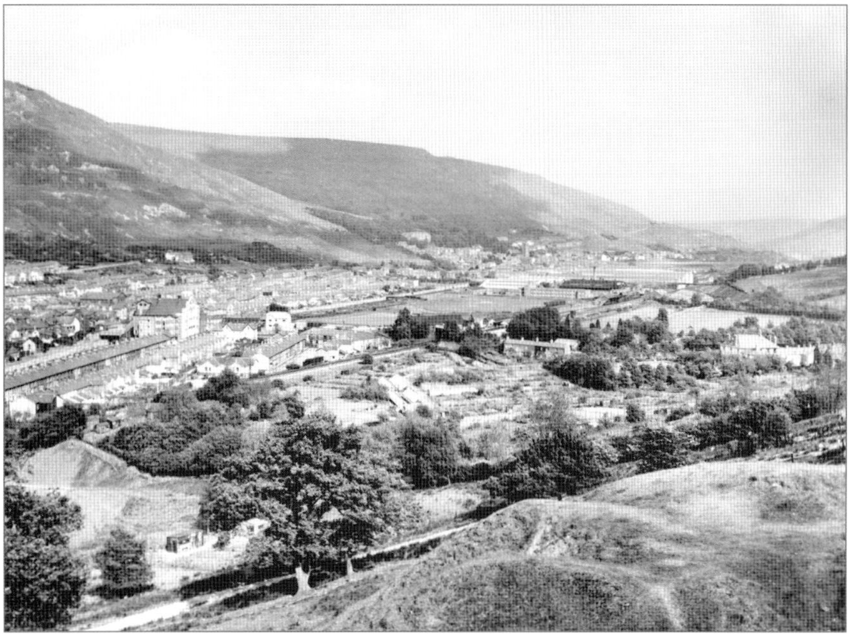

◄ **TREORCHY**
The Rhondda Valley Looking South c1955
T197049

Of all the general views this one shows the topography of the Rhondda in the best detail. The town stretches out along the valley floor; the gentle rise on this side shows the fertility of the clay soil producing the growth of greenery whilst the mountains in the distance reflect the resistance to the development of any growth. This shows rows of terraced miners' cottages, especially on the left. In the centre are extensive allotments, and behind them the rugby ground.

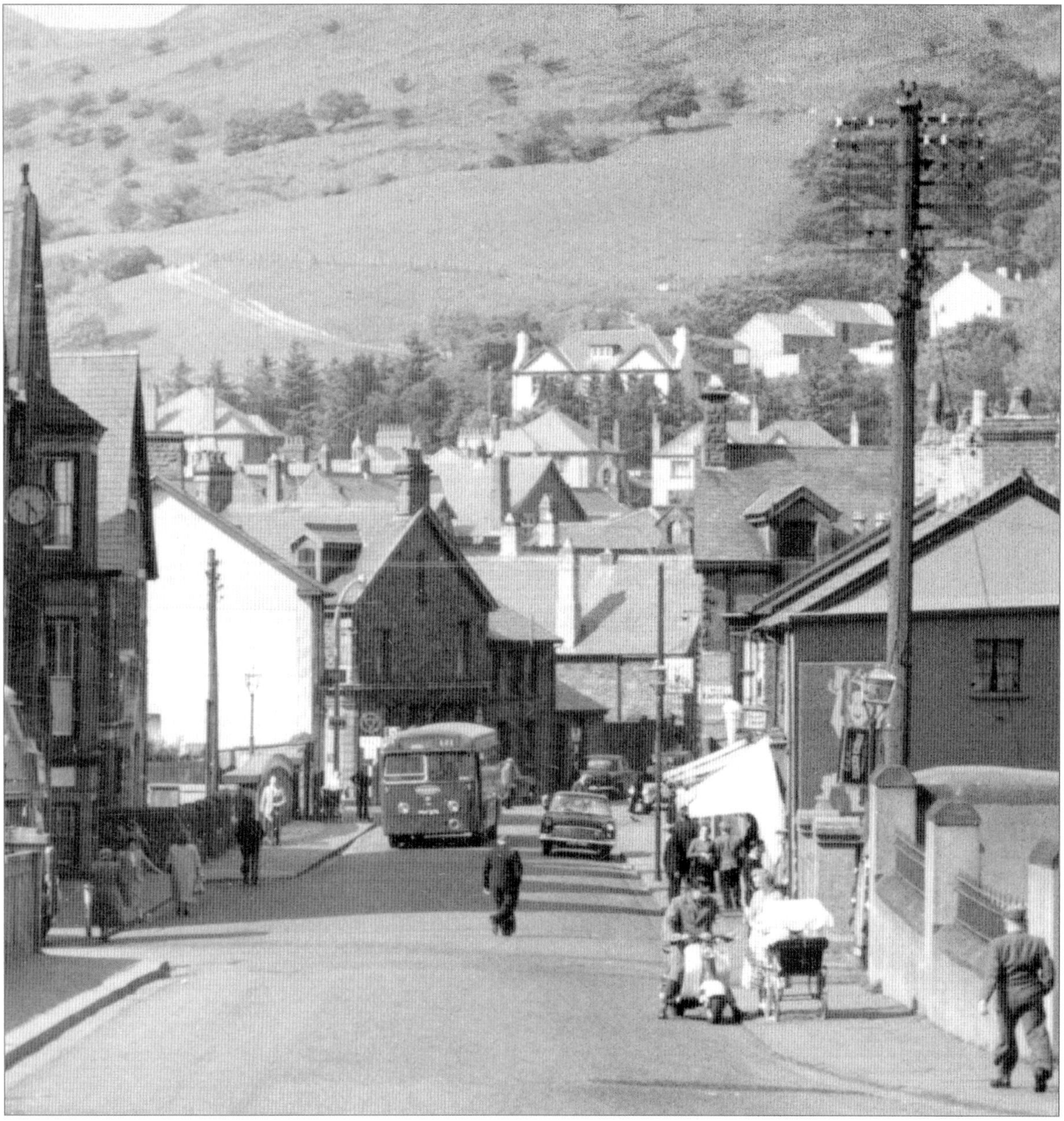

TREORCHY

Station Road c1960 T197050a

Plenty of activity is perceivable in this narrow road leading to the station. A single decker bus is passing a parked car whilst a double decker waits to join Station Road and a moped rider chats to a friend with pram. Alongside the single decker a gable end hoarding advertises Timothy Whites and Taylor, a chemist's chain that once rivalled Boots. Cigarette advertising is now totally banned but in 1960s Treorchy there are adverts for 'Players' and 'Capstan' on the shops and 'Woodbines' on the bus!

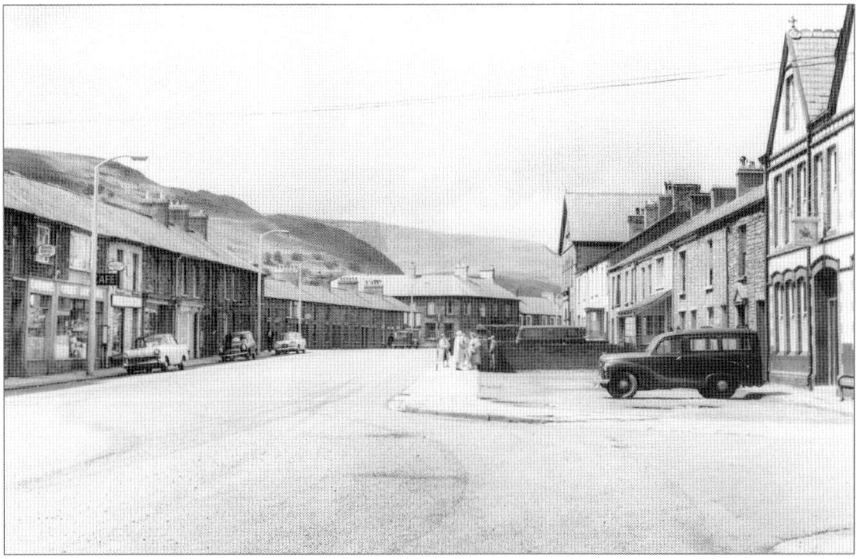

TREORCHY
Bute Street c1965 T197073

Owing to the topographical restriction, most of the town and villages along the valley of the Rhondda had but one main street that ran the length of the locale. And as we have seen it was invariably 'Bute Street'. This is no exception and its width gives it an air of grandeur. A Morris van, probably with windows added later to avoid a higher purchase tax, is neatly reversed against the hotel selling 'Rhymney Beers'. Across the street a variety of shops includes a café and chemist's.

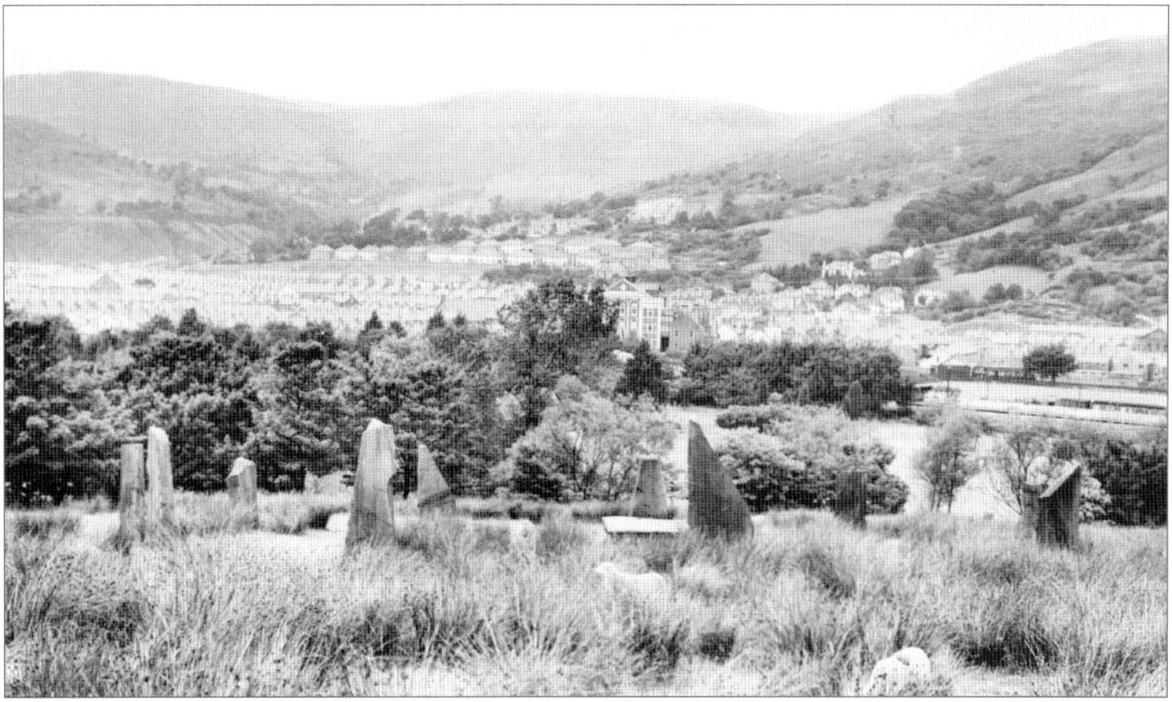

TREORCHY, *The Gorsedd Circle c1955* T197060

Stone circles are a common sight in all Celtic lands, especially Wales and Cornwall, but those in Wales are not always prehistoric: many were built in modern times, or after a particularly distinguished eistedfodd, a festival of music and poetry. The circle pictured here was erected when the National Eistedfodd was held here in 1928.

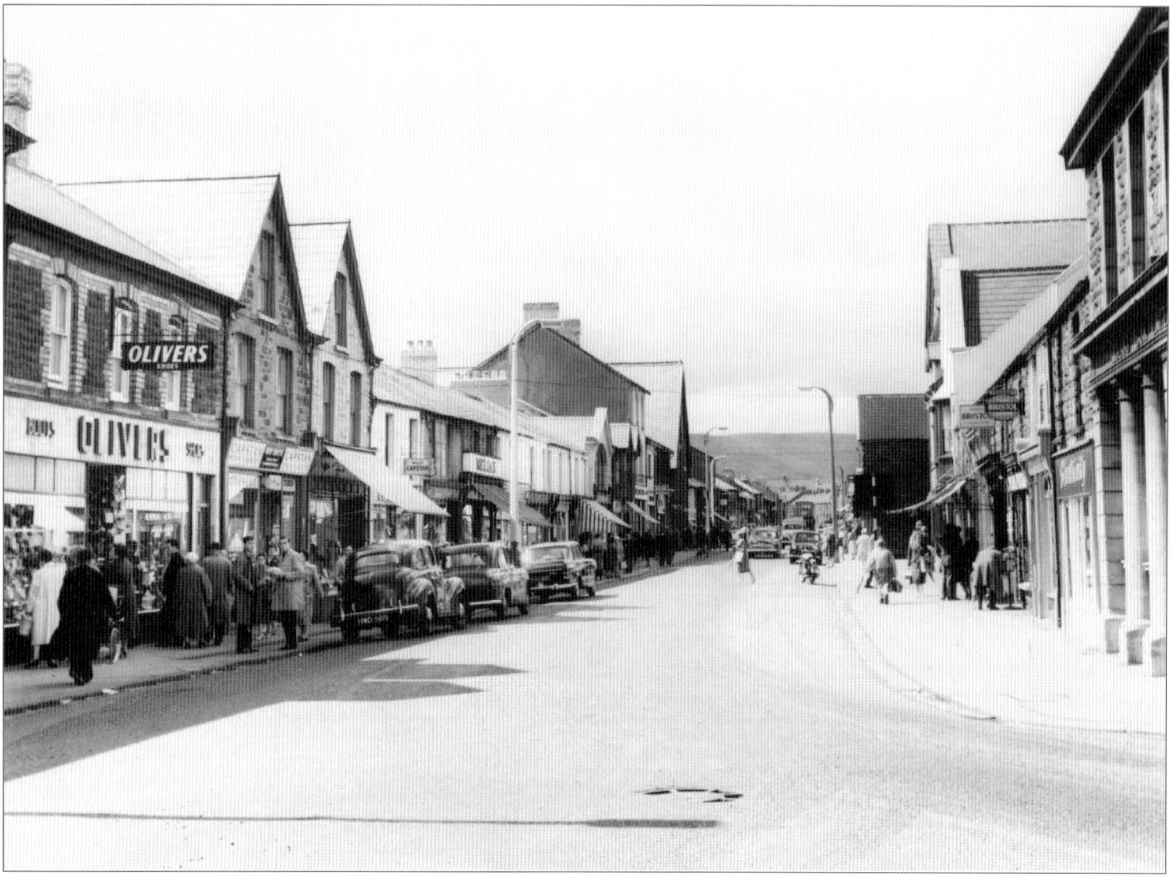

TREORCHY

High Street c1965 T197080

Lloyd's Bank with its recurrent columns takes pride of place on the right hand corner here, with 'Olivers' store directly opposite. Various cars, mainly Morris and Ford, glisten in the sun.

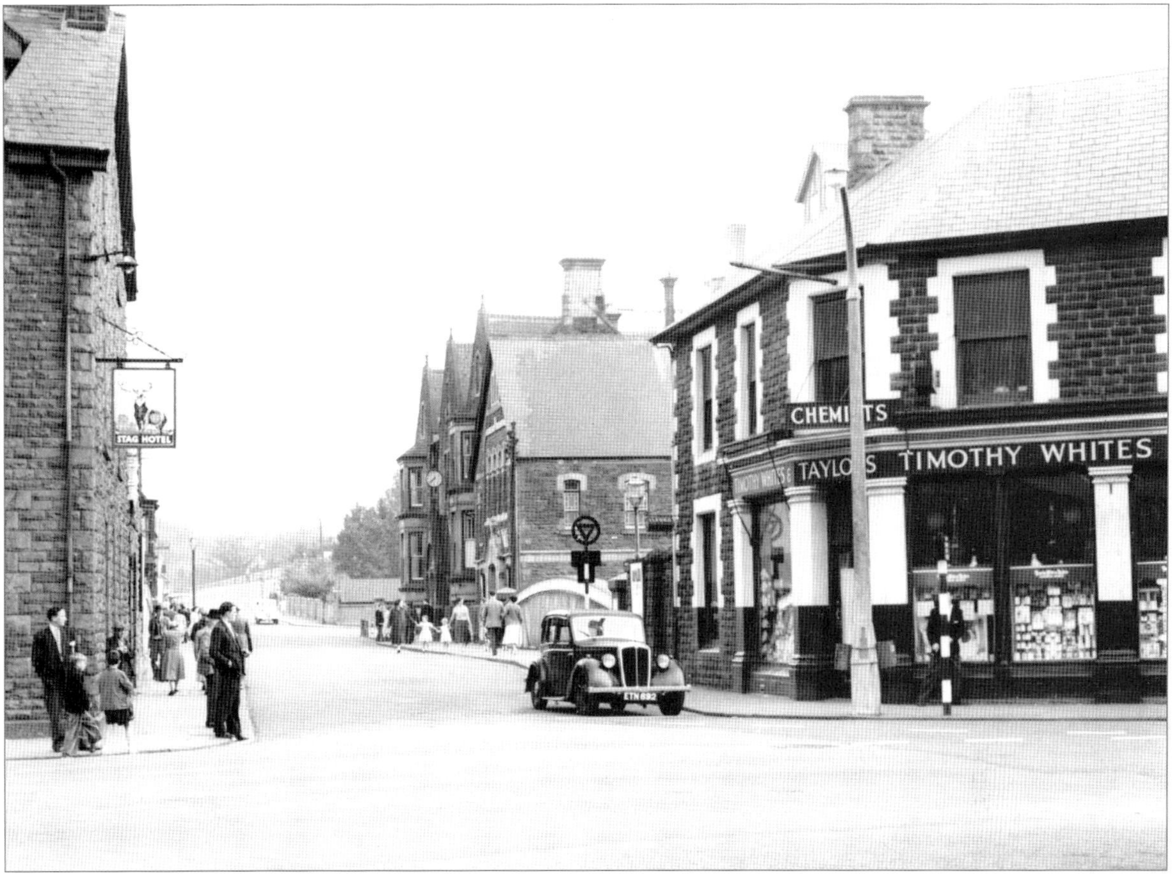

TREORCHY

The Square c1955 T197067

Timothy Whites, the chemist shop seen on the right of this view, was once a familiar sight in many towns. The chain was taken over by Boots the Chemist in 1968.

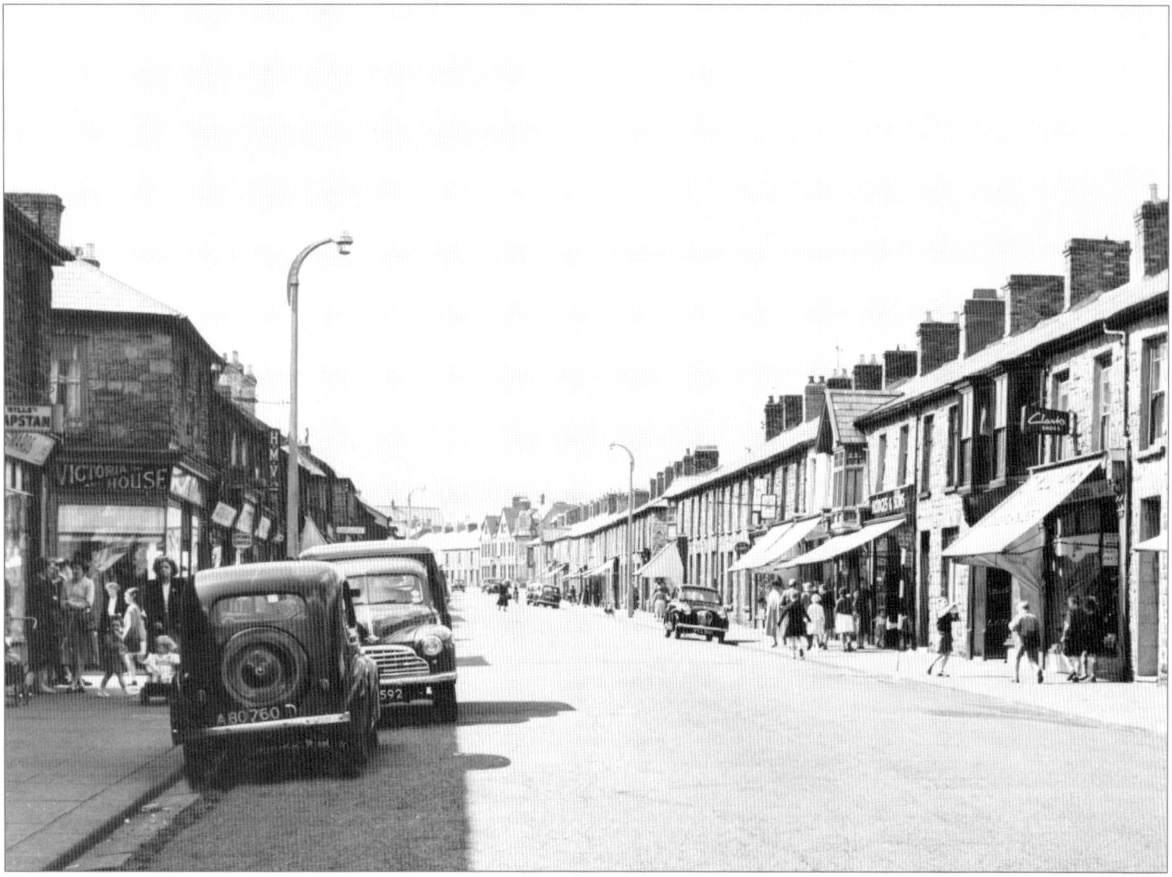

TREORCHY

High Street c1955 T197042

Plenty of people are out and about here, including a group of children outside the shoe shop. There are many product advertisements of commodities we still buy today - 'Clarks shoes', 'Lyon's Cakes' and the inevitable 'Wills Capstan'. A Morris 1000 van faces the camera in the foreground whilst an Austin A35 rests further down the street.

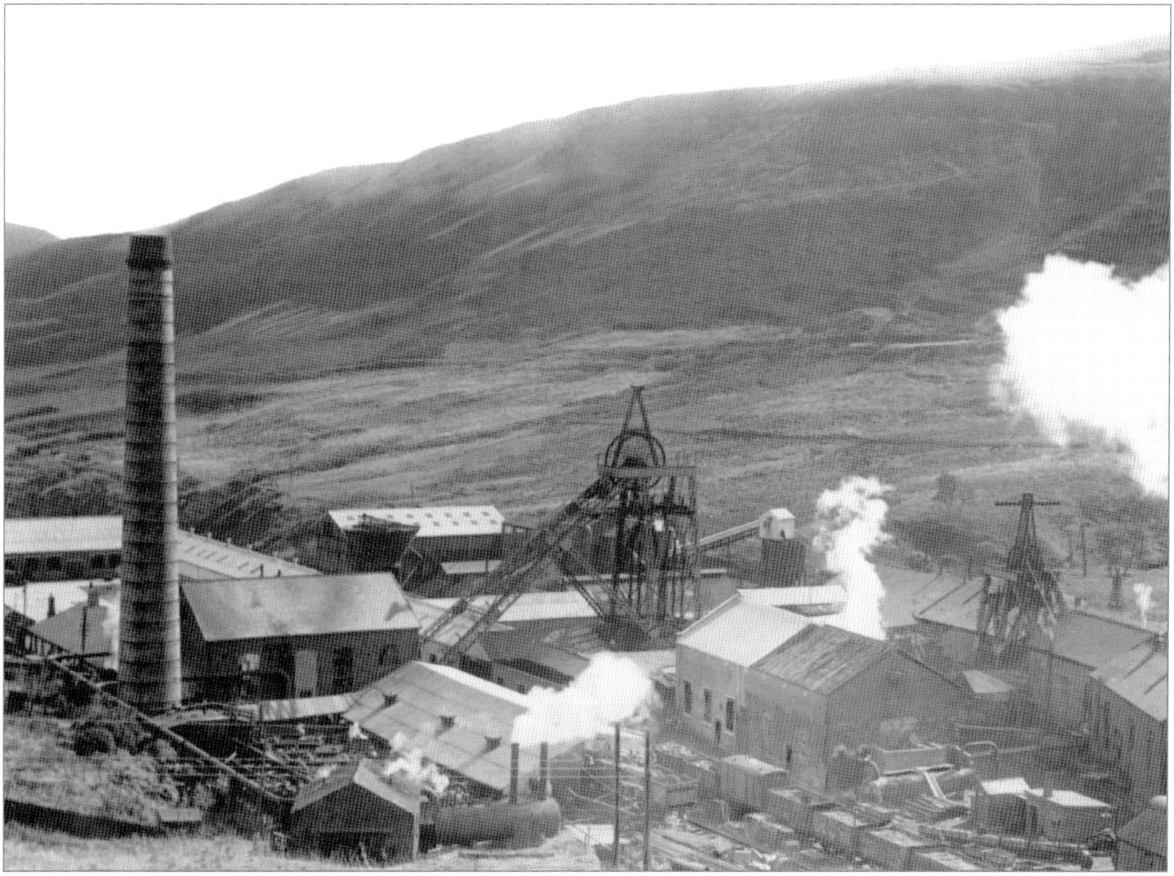

CWMPARC

Parc Pit c1955 C391005

This small area had some of the best coal in the Rhondda and in addition to the mighty Parc Pit (seen here) there was also the Dare Colliery. This latter was sunk in 1866 and by 1890 was producing 184,000 tons of coal per year, from a workforce of 748 men and boys. It finally closed in February 1964.

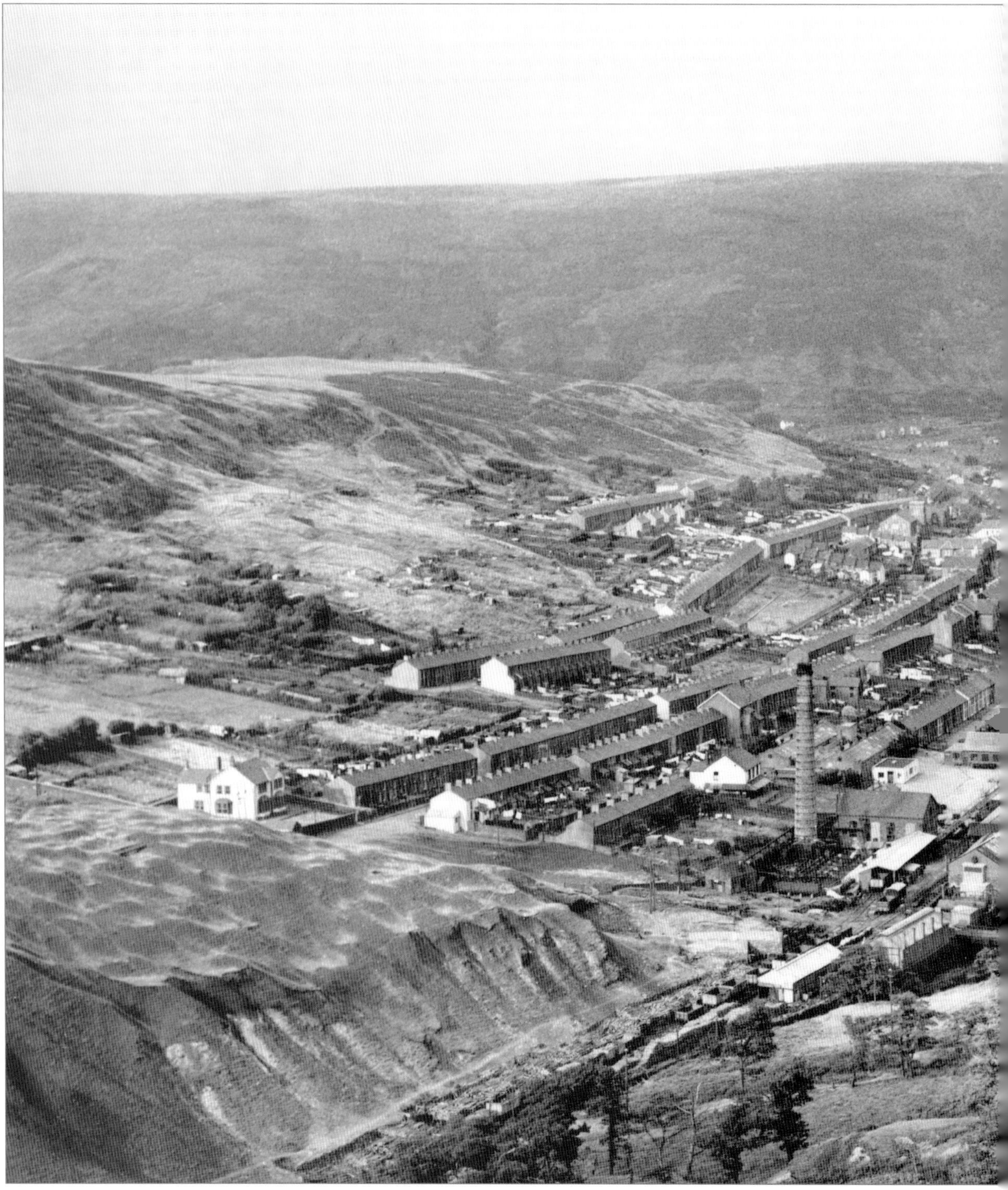

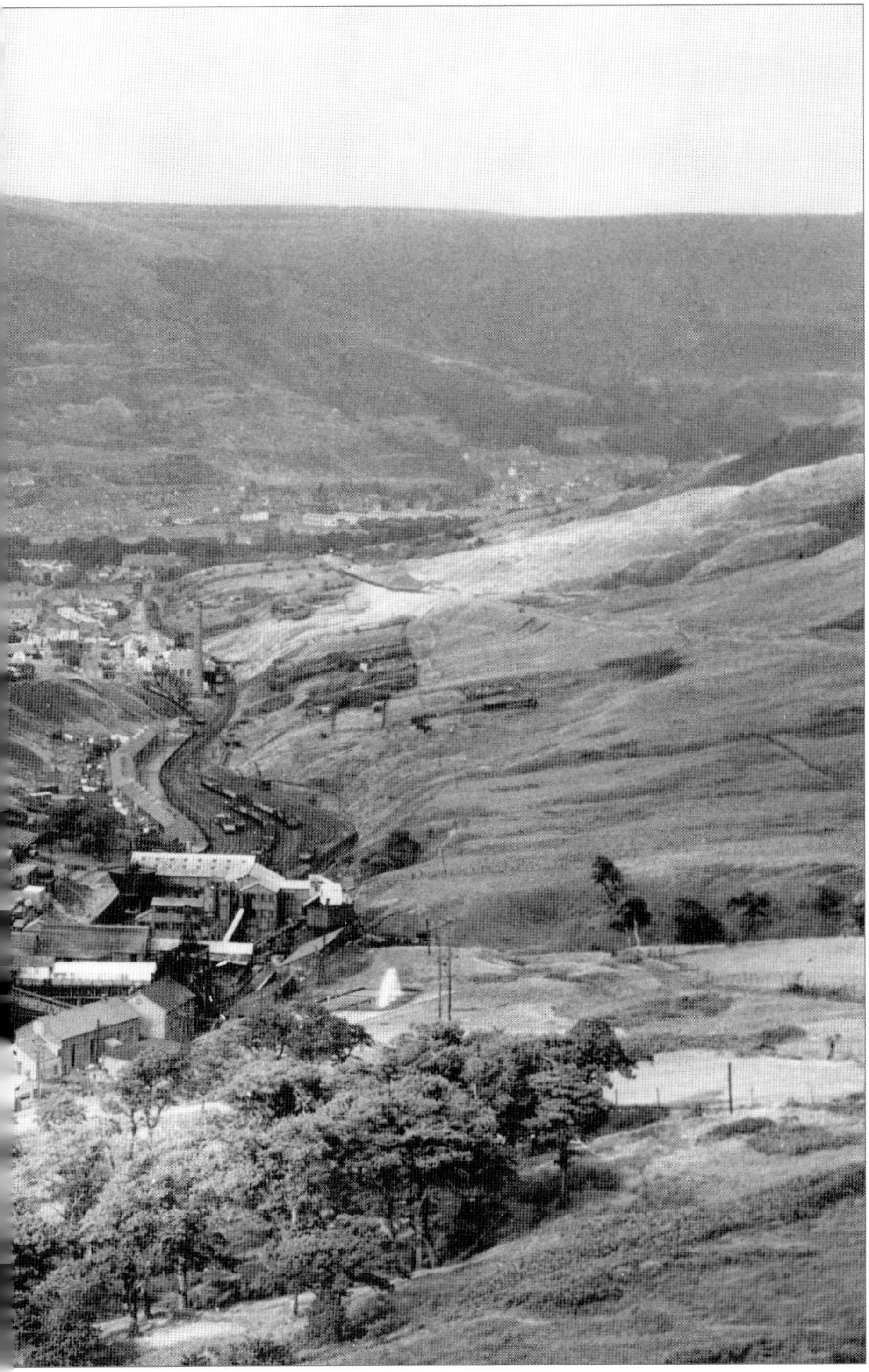

CWMPARC

Upper Cwmparc from Mountain Road c1960

C391008

As a memory of the heady days of 'King Coal', this picture has everything. From the sweeping mountain heights to the massive Parc Pit controlling all around, the miners' terraced cottages are dwarfed by the colliery workings. From the slagheaps in the left foreground to the winding shafts in the centre, the railway snakes along the valley floor, its wagons awaiting their precious lode - and load.

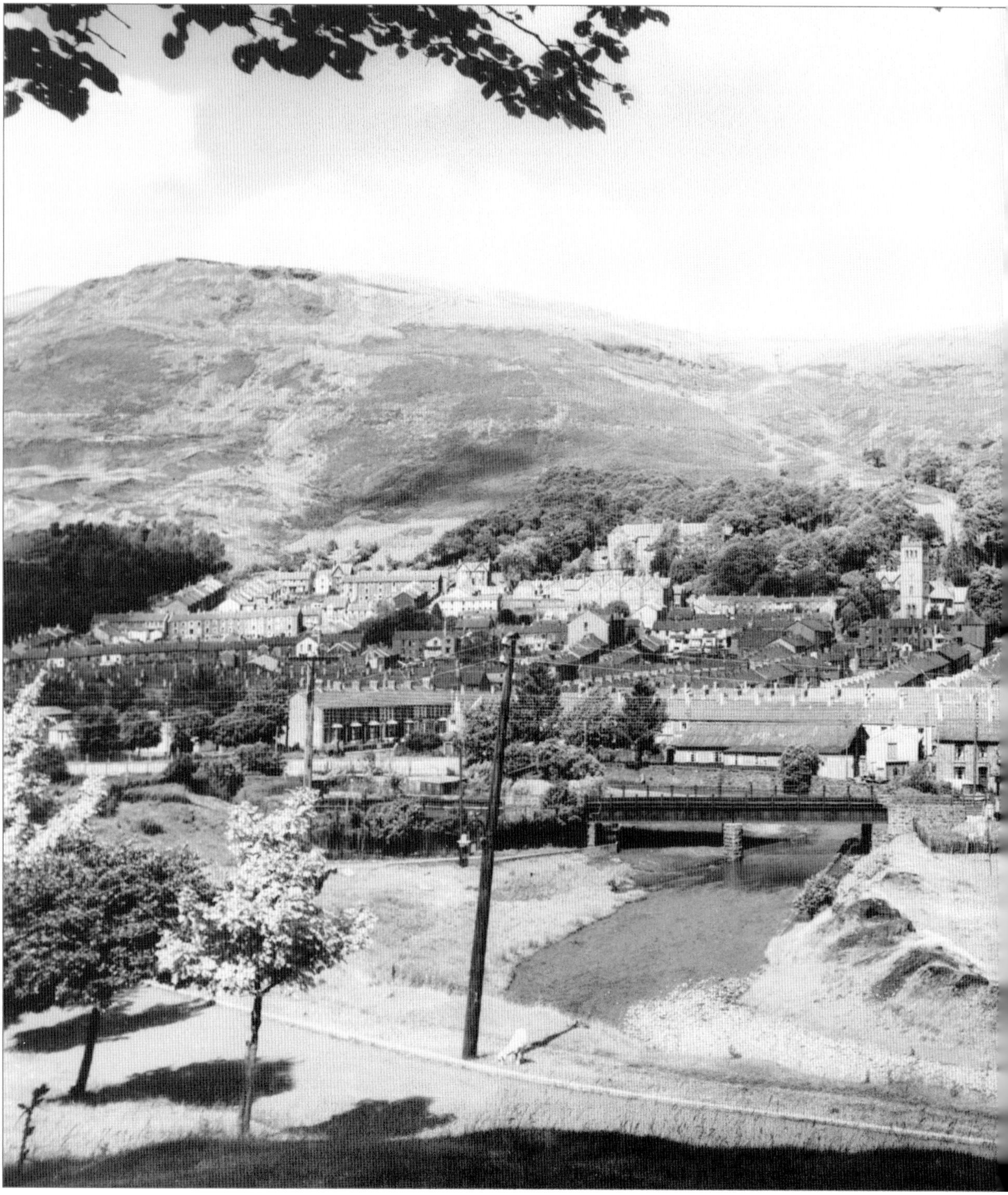

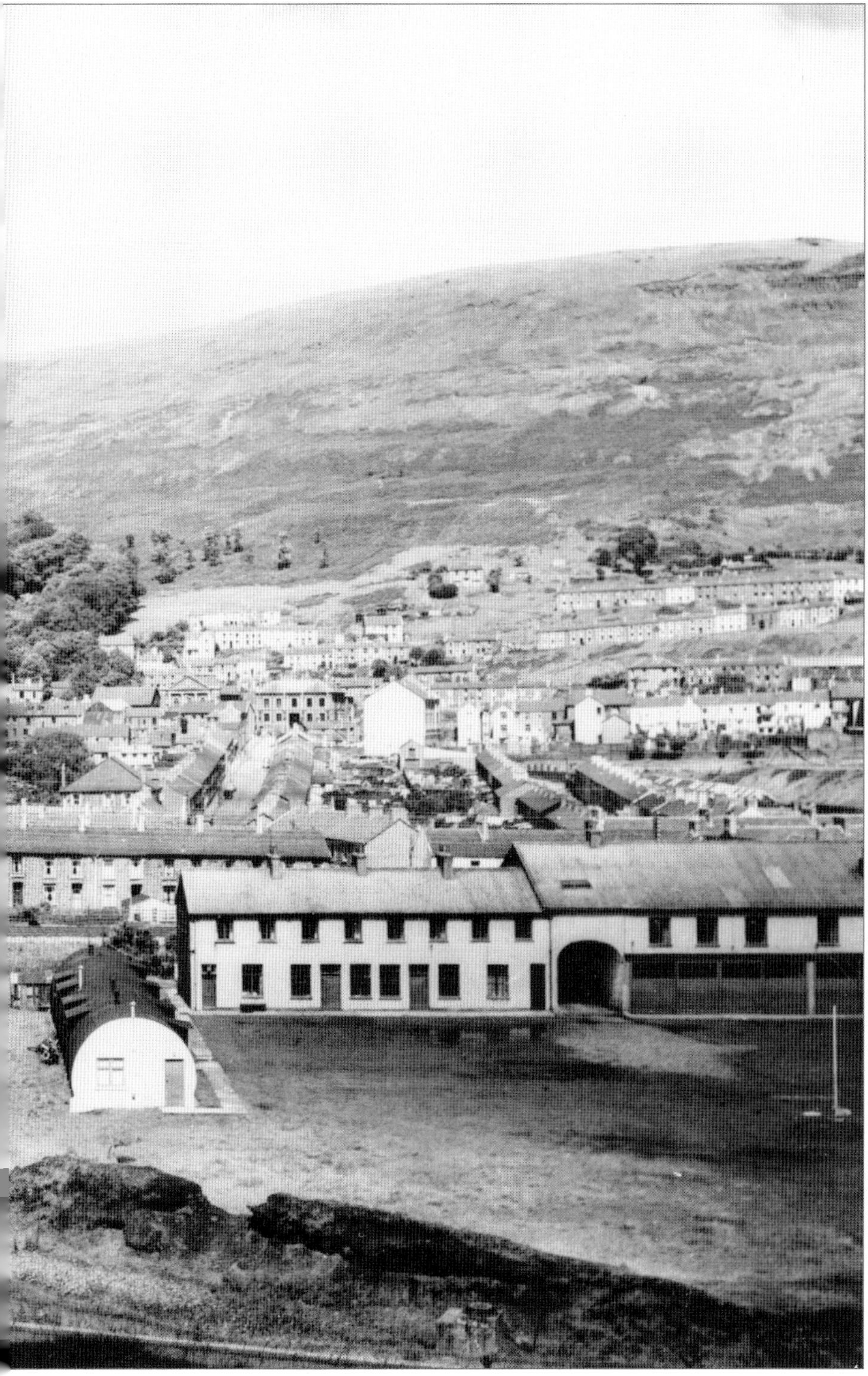

PENTRE
General View c1965
P225006

Moving ever southward, this is the town of Pentre which has similarities to the previous localities in terms of the huddled terraced housing, but for the first time the Rhondda Fawr can be seen. The line of the river can be clearly picked up by the woodland growth in the centre adjacent to the church. The river runs under the Railway Bridge before swinging away to the right in the near foreground.

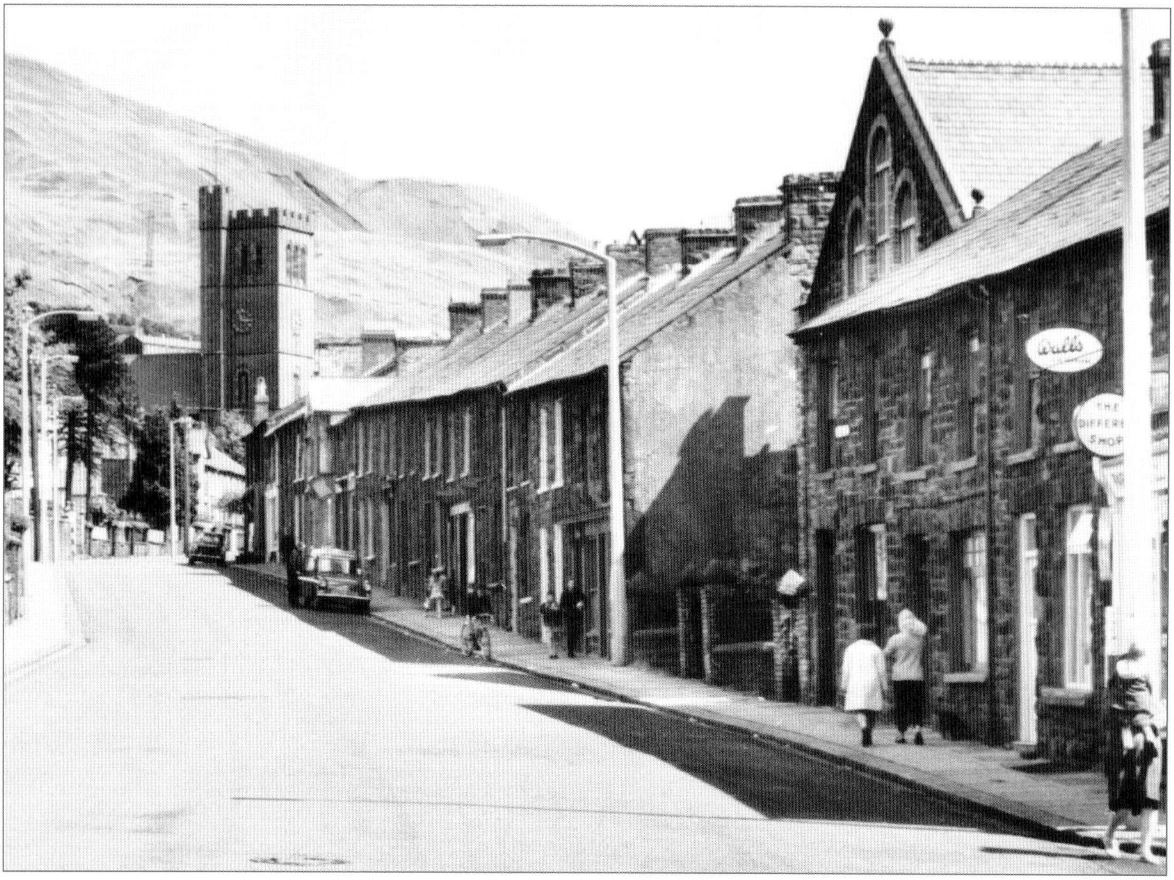

PENTRE

Carne Street c1965 P225003a

Dominating the centre of the town is St Peter's Church, built between 1888 and 1890 and a good example of 'Early English Style'. The tower is 100 feet high and accommodates eight bells. Carne Street has now got electric lighting and has a pleasant mix of pedestrians, cyclists and car drivers. 'Walls' ice cream is sold at what could be 'The Different Shop' - if the sign was not partially obscured by lighting standard.

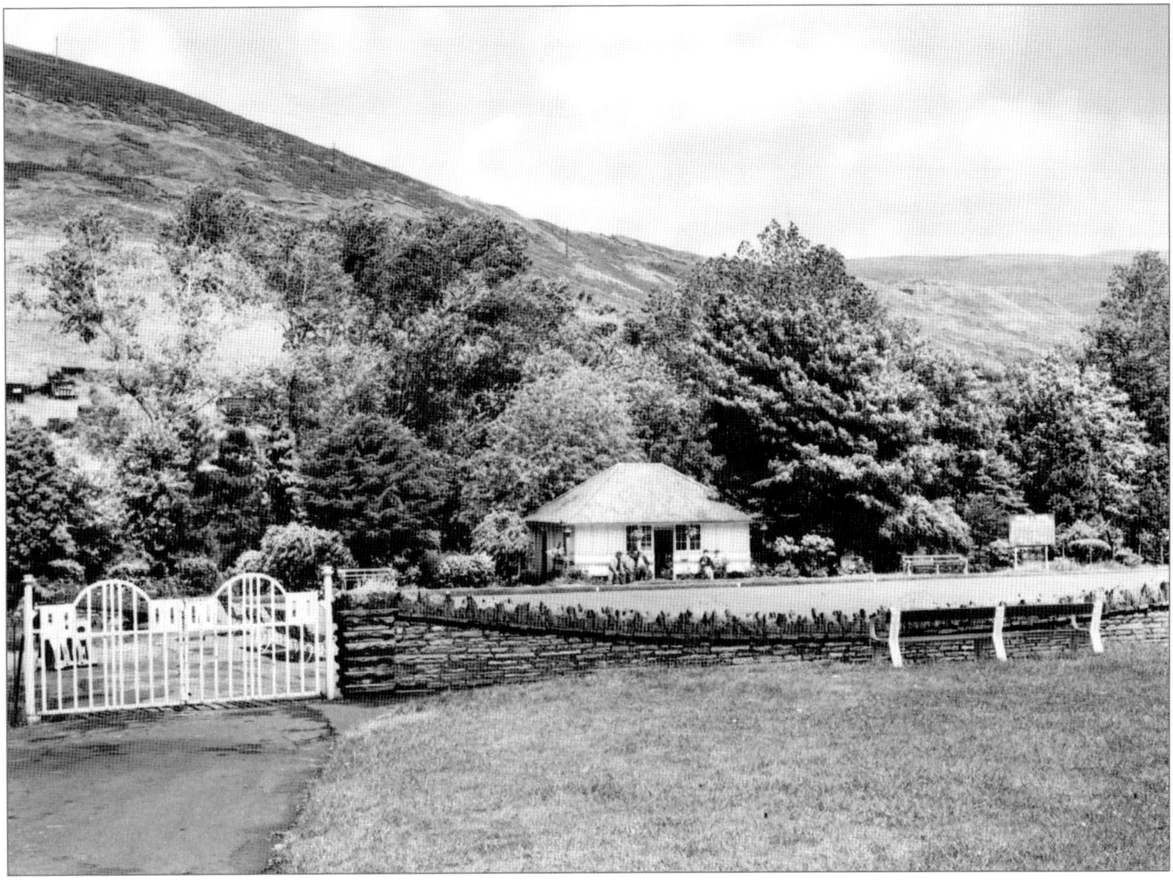

TON PENTRE

Gelli Park c1955 T191002

A most pleasing aspect to the bowling green and hut is neatly enclosed by a fine wrought-iron gate and highly unusual boundary wall sloping away to the centre, giving a full view to the 'outsiders'.

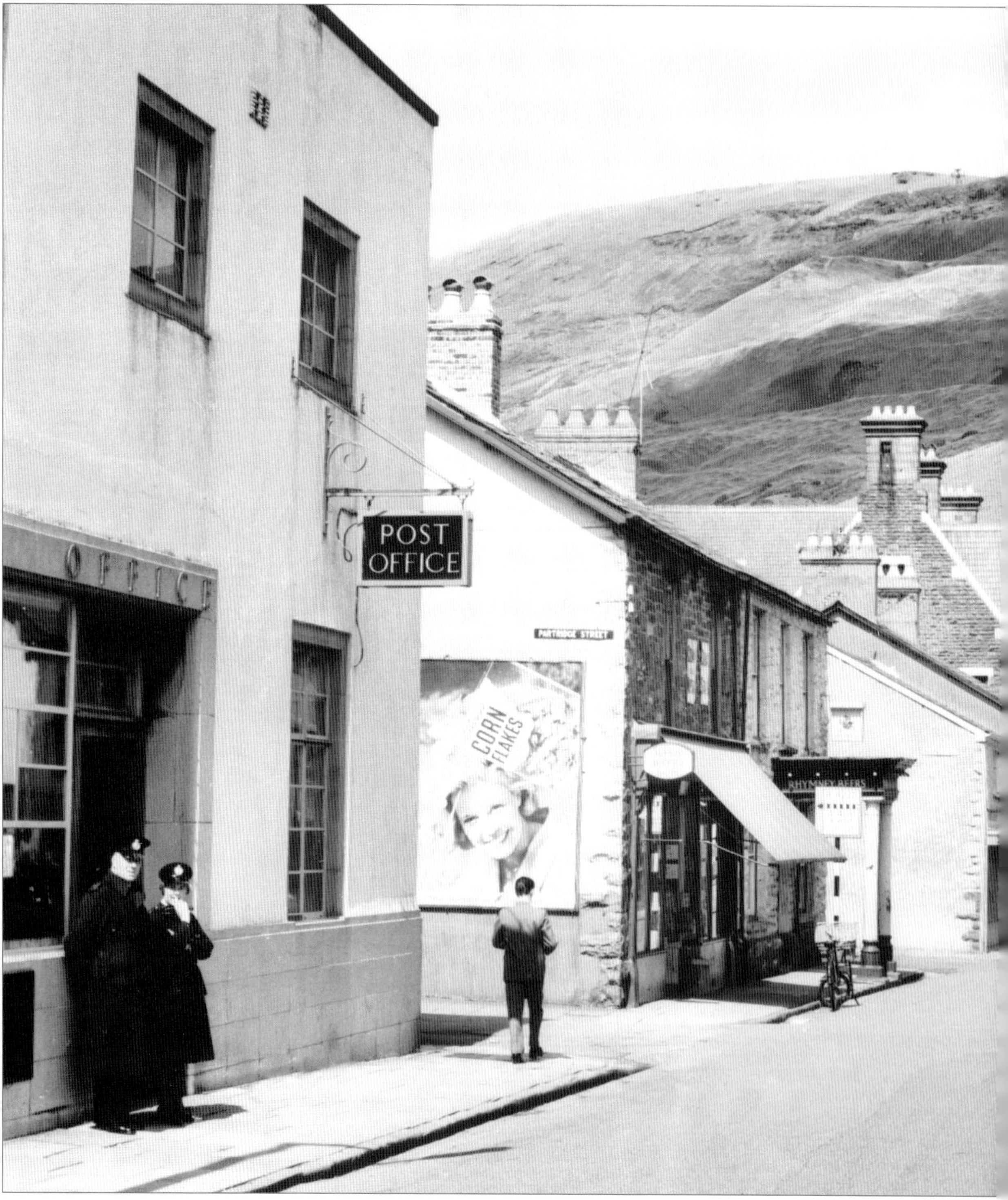
OFFICE
POST
OFFICE
CORN
FLAKES

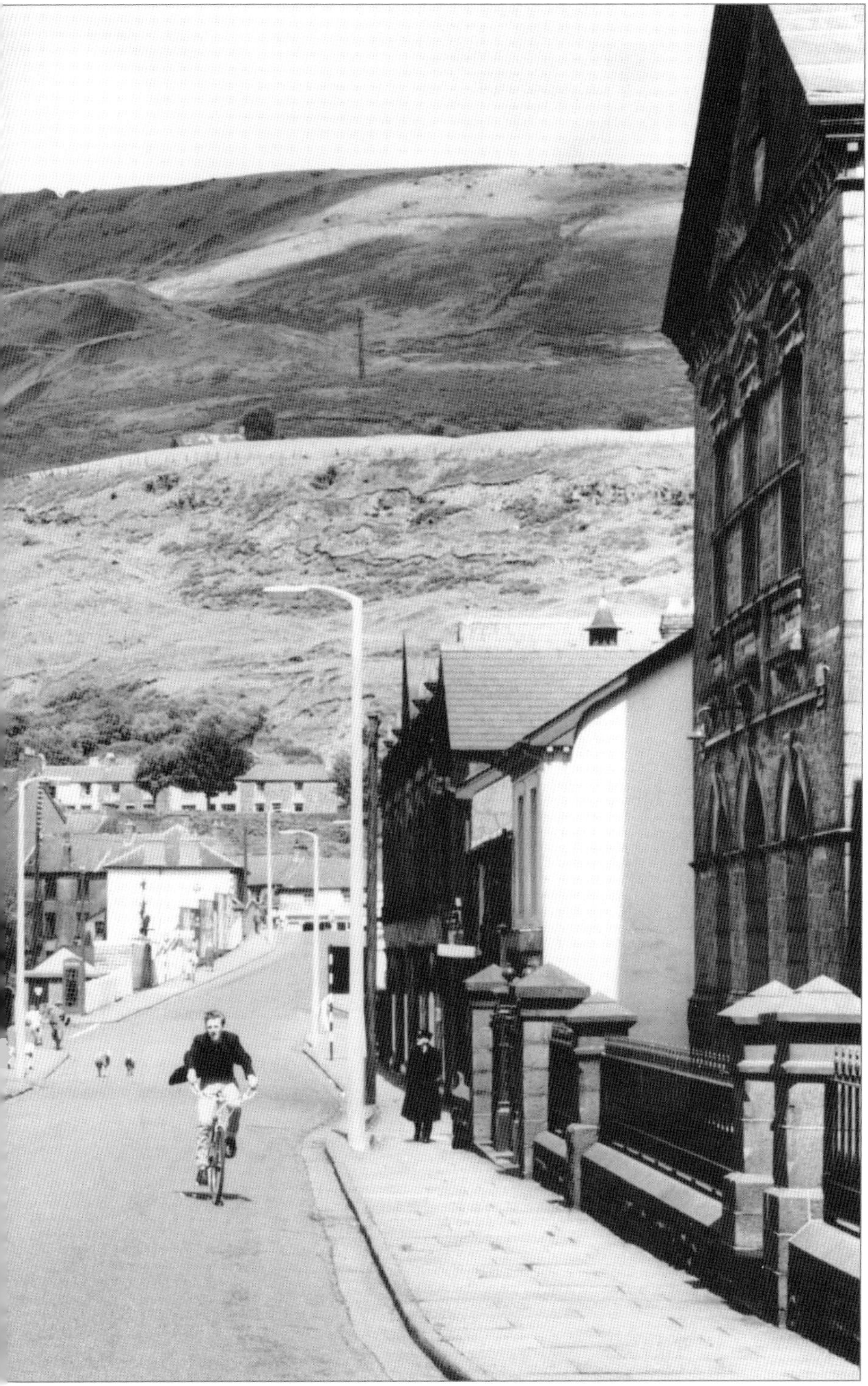

TON PENTRE
Church Road c1955
T191008

One of the biggest crowds ever to have gathered in the Rhondda watched a football match between Mid-Rhondda and Ton Pentre in 1919. The event, held in Tonypandy, was a preliminary round of the FA Cup tournament. One of the Mid-Rhondda players was Jimmy Steel, who later played for England at International level. He recalled the event in his autobiography: 'The rivalry was terrific and there was little else discussed in the miners' pubs and clubs a week before the match…the mountainside overlooking the field was black with spectators who couldn't get inside… believe me, there was more excitement from this huge crowd than any huge gathering I have since witnessed at Wembley, Hampden Park, Ninian Park or Windsor Park.' Over 20,000 people saw Ton Pentre win the match.

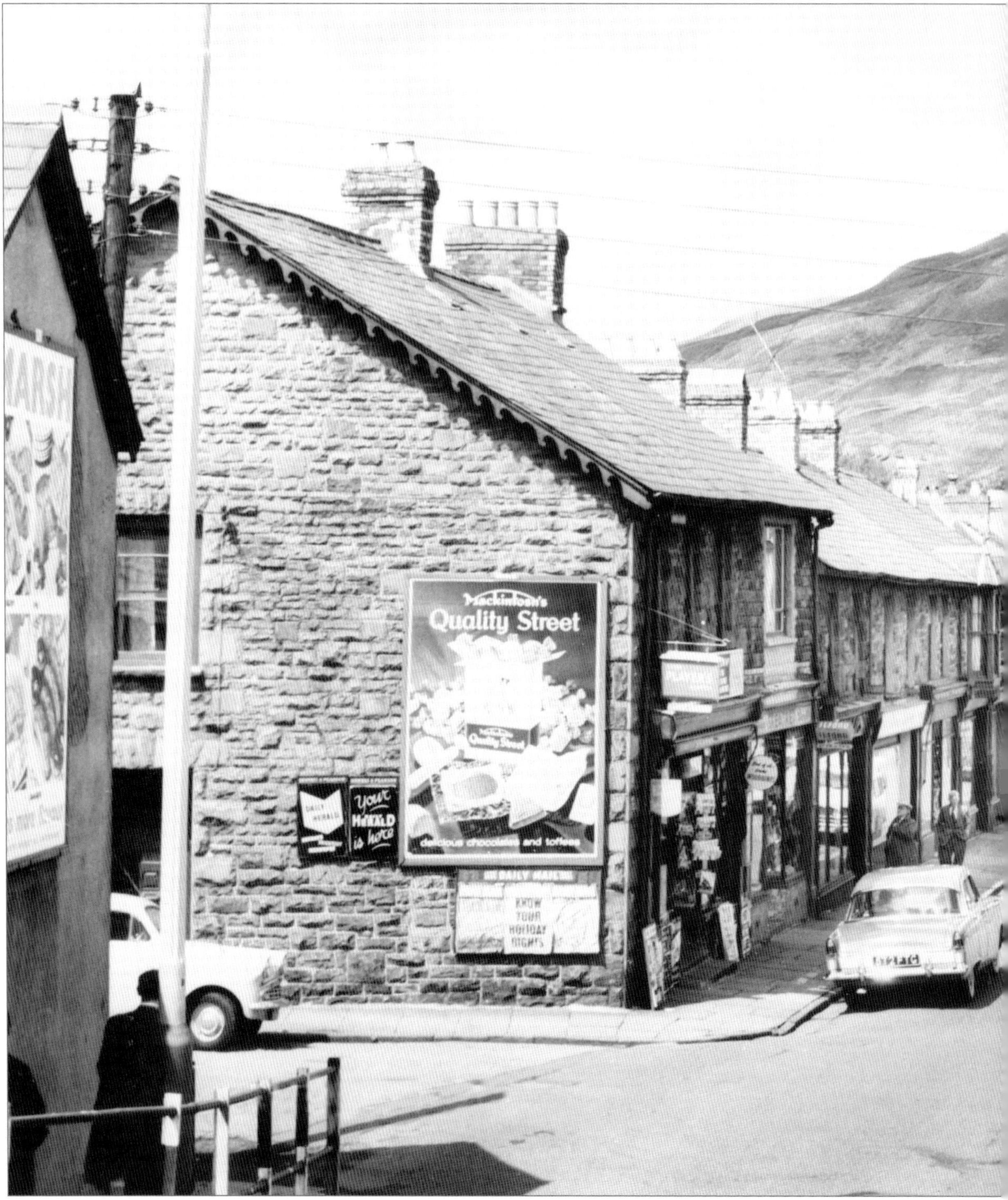
Mackintosh's
Quality Street
delicious chocolates and toffees
Your HERALD is here
DAILY MAIL
KNOW YOUR HOLIDAY RIGHTS

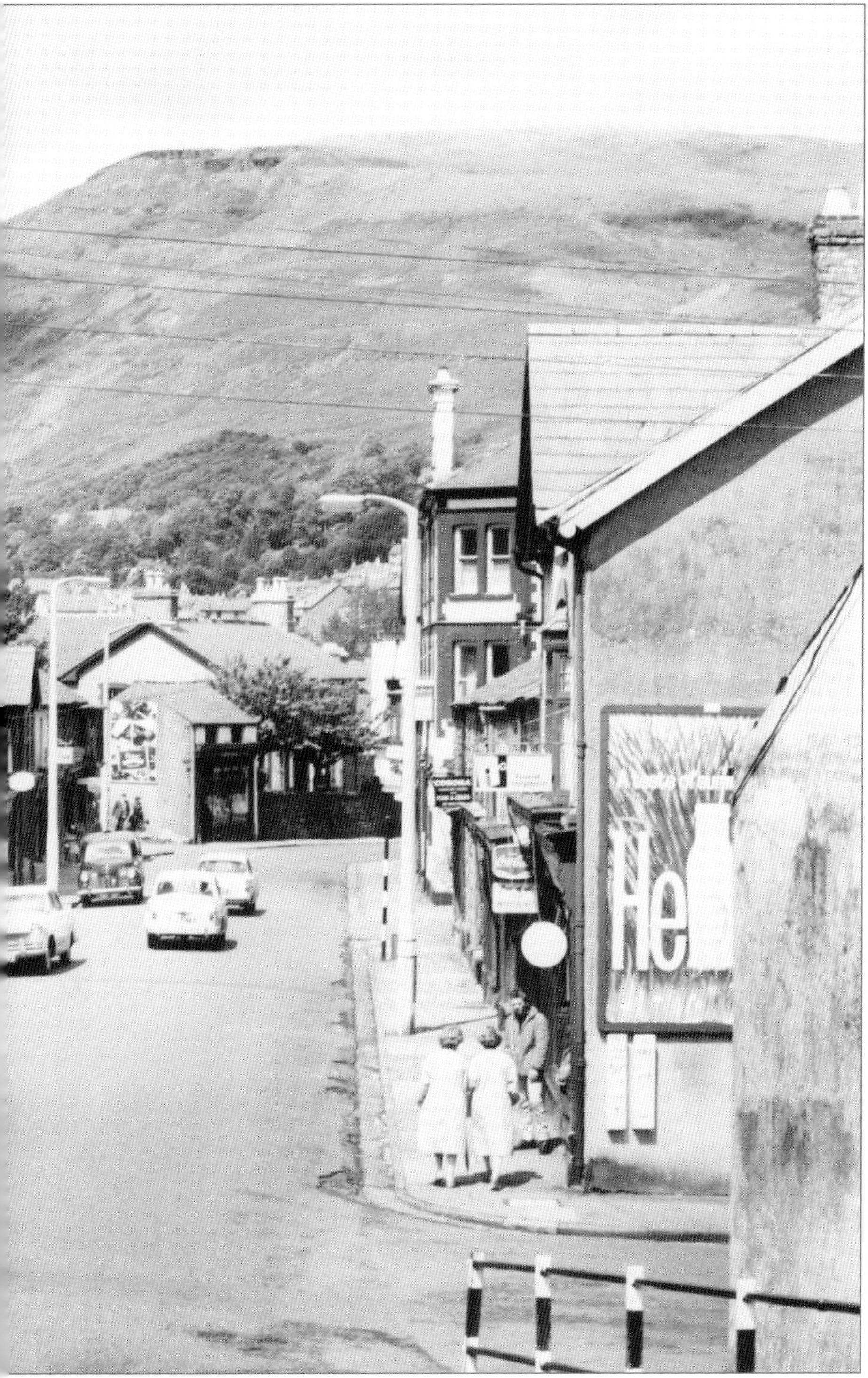

TON PENTRE
Church Road c1960
T191001

A gleaming and expensive Ford Zephyr/Zodiac is parked around the corner from a small billboard with the slogan; 'Your Daily Herald is here'. The 'Daily Herald' until its demise in March 1961 was the last radical Labour-supporting newspaper, to be replaced by the 'Daily Mirror'.

TON PENTRE, *Ystrad Road c1955* T191010

The building has a rather unusual feature in that the ground floors are rendered, above which the upper storeys are stone. It seems to be right across the road from the station and a little further along is a Vauxhall garage - but with no Vauxhall in sight!

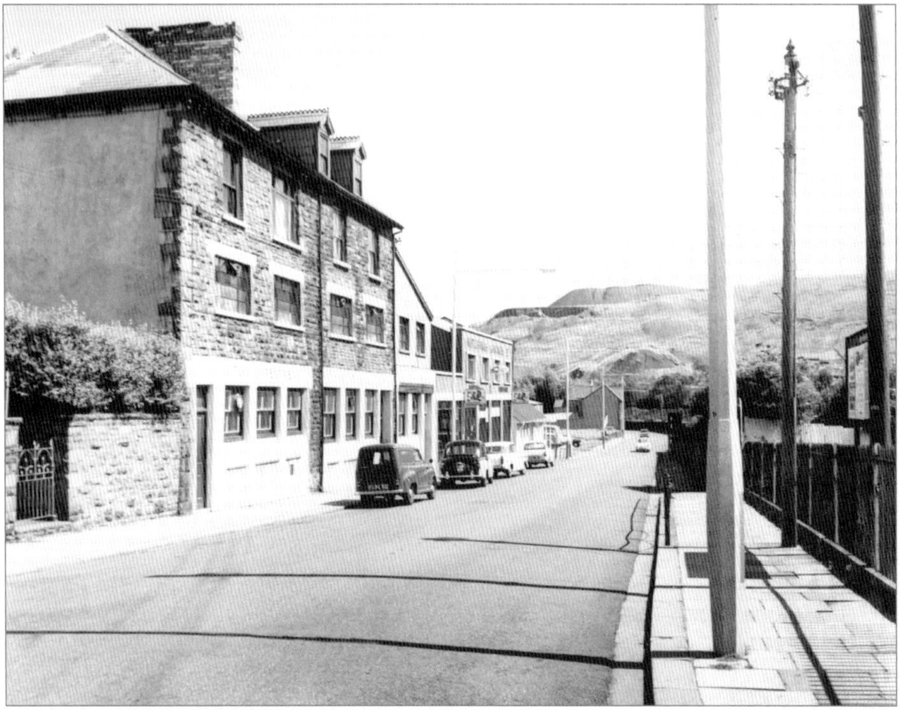

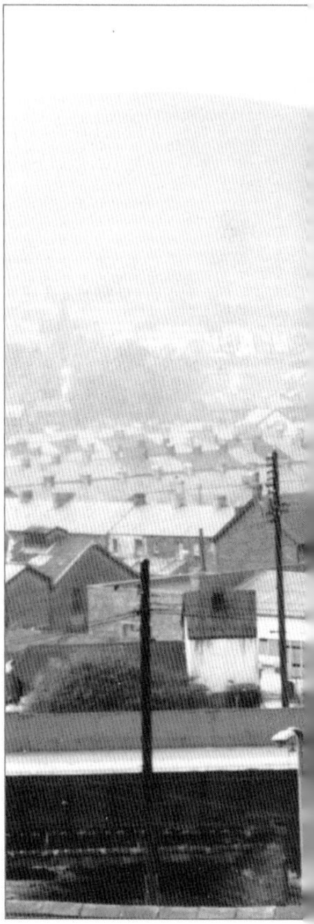

TON PENTRE

The Rhondda Fawr Valley c1965 T191021

Looking east across the Rhondda Fawr Valley to the corresponding heights of Pentre. The smallest miners' terraces are in the valley bottom whereas the larger and newer houses are on the higher ground.

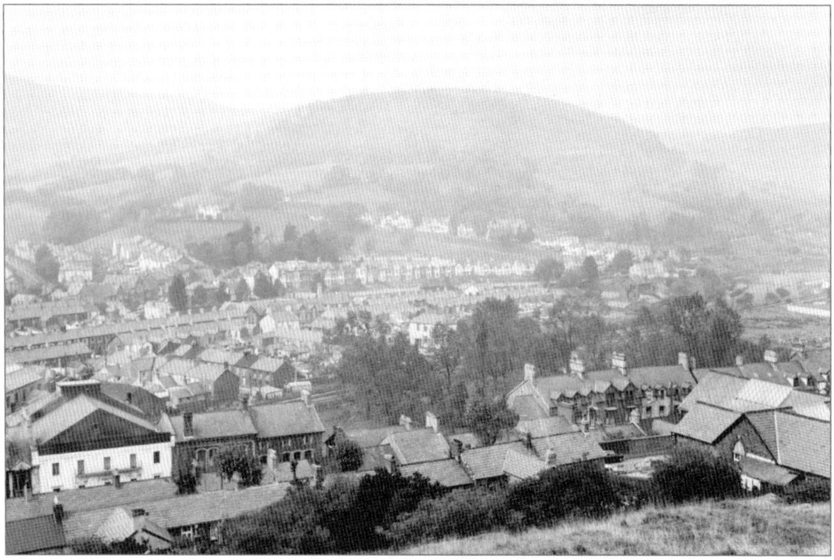

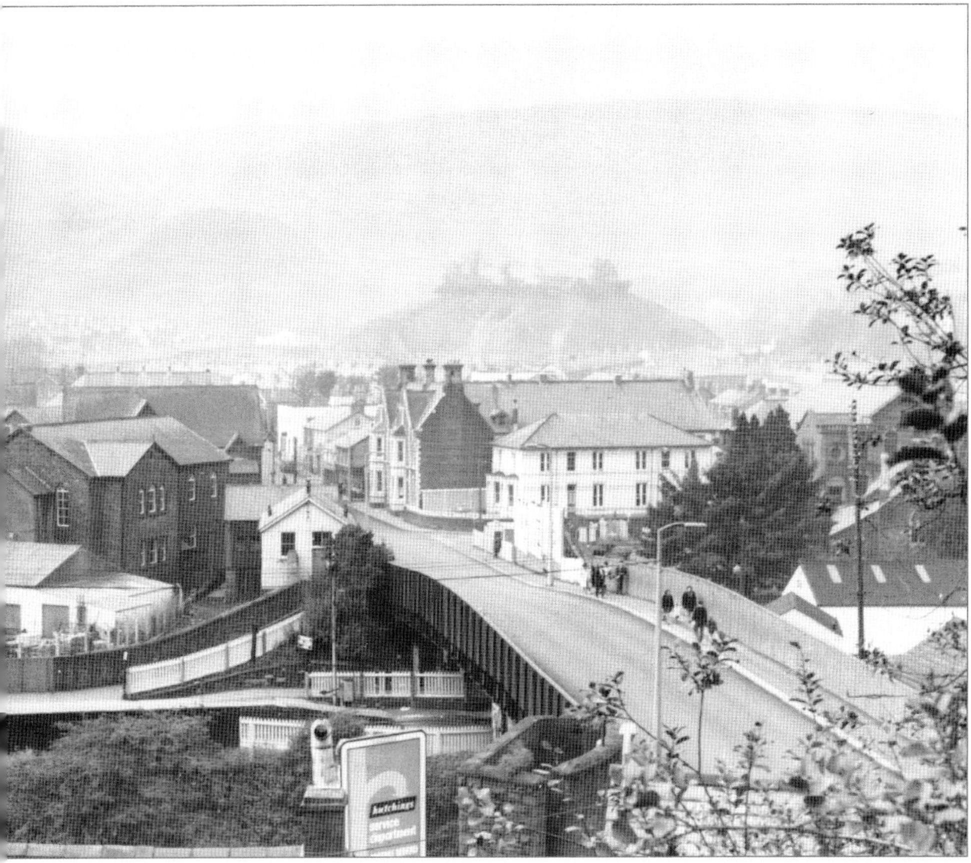

TON PENTRE
The Rhondda Fawr Valley c1960 T191019

The road bridge arches ever so slightly to cross the railway line and the sign in the foreground advertises 'Hutchings Service Department'. The vagueness of the background mountains is probably low cloud or even early-morning mist.

YSTRAD
General View c1955
Y28004

The B4512 sweeps down steeply to Ystrad. As the meaning of 'Ystrad' is simply 'valley' it is no surprise that there are many towns throughout Wales with the prefix 'Ystrad'. To differentiate this one its full Welsh title is 'Ystradyfodwg', or in English, 'Ystradrhondda'.

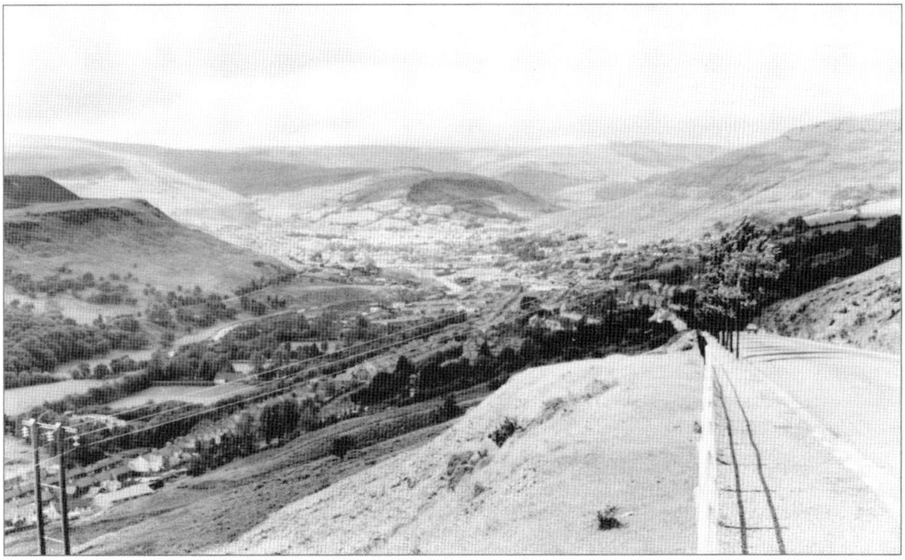

▼ **YSTRAD,** *Nantwyddon Road c1960* Y28005b

'Nantwyddon' is a tiny place, but there was a deep pit there in 1860. In this photo it seems a most pleasing and peaceful avenue with the mature woodland to one side and modern street lighting on the opposite side.

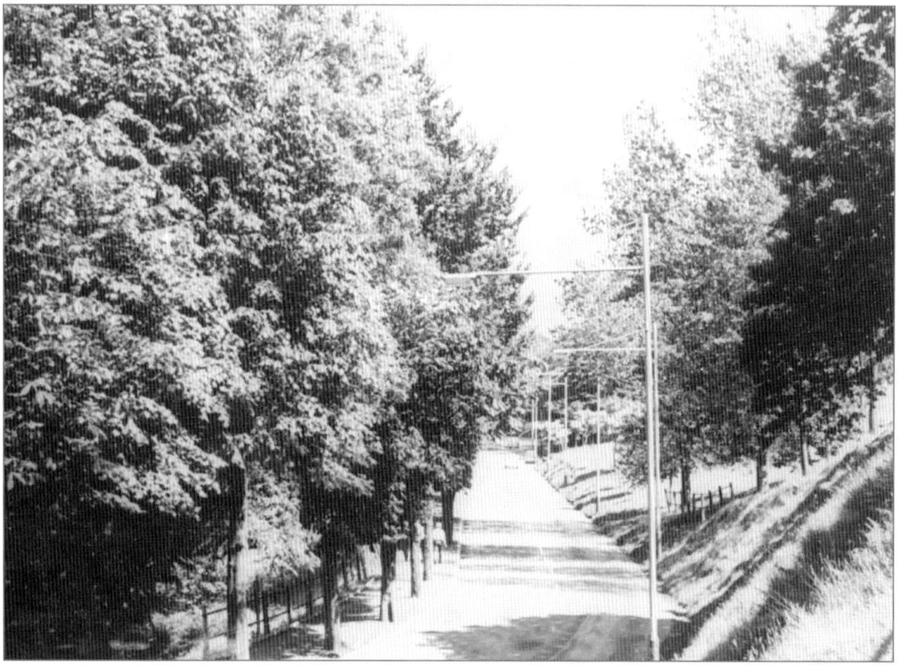

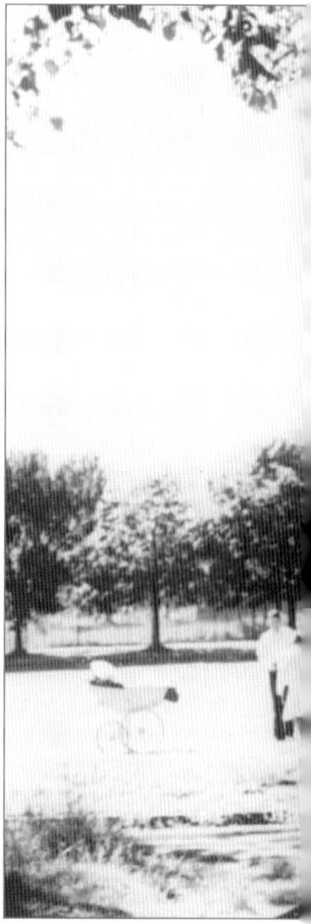

► **YSTRAD**
Gelligaled Road c1960
Y28005c

Of the meanings of 'gelli' it would be reasonable to assume that its meaning here was 'colliery'. It would seem to be primarily a residential area with what appears to be a general store in the centre right. A young couple with pram can just be seen alongside a large saloon, a Ford or even a Humber.

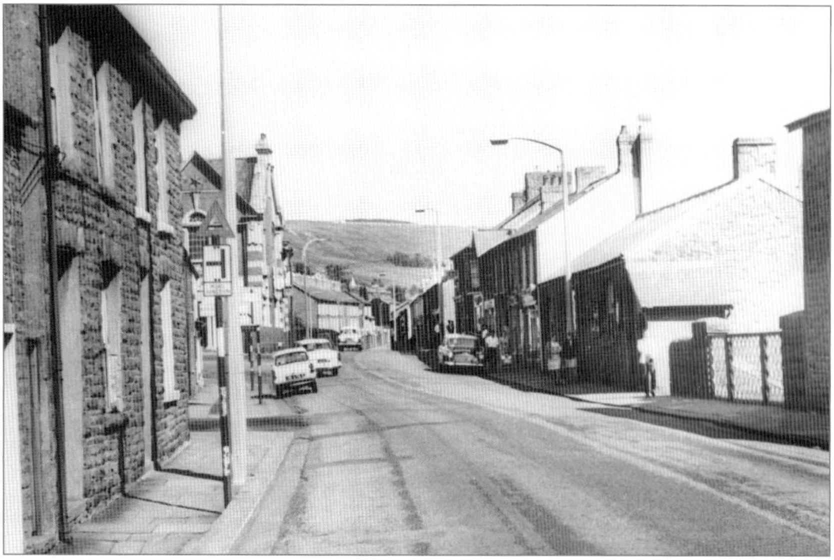

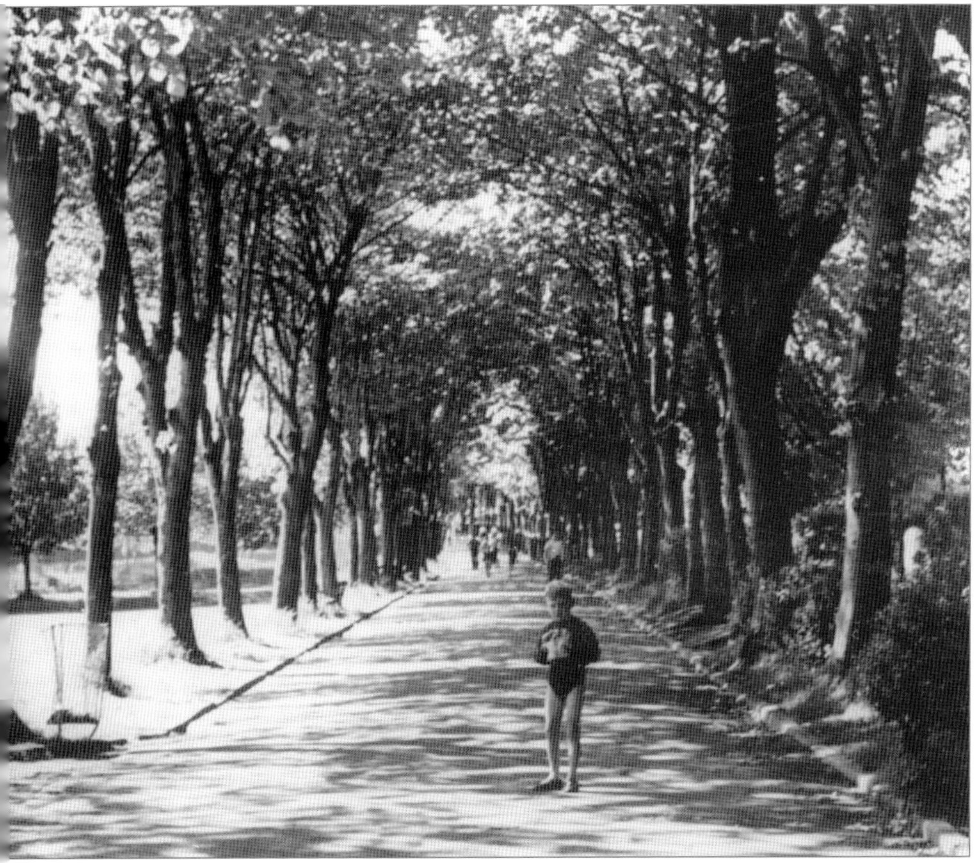

YSTRAD
Long Walk, Gelligaled Park c1960 Y28005d

The group on the grass seem to have the most prestigious pram of the time - the 'Silver Cross' - made in Guiseley, Yorkshire.

YSTRAD
The Paddling Pool c1960 Y28005a

Part of Gelligaled Park is given over to a children's paddling pool with plenty of seating for the parents.

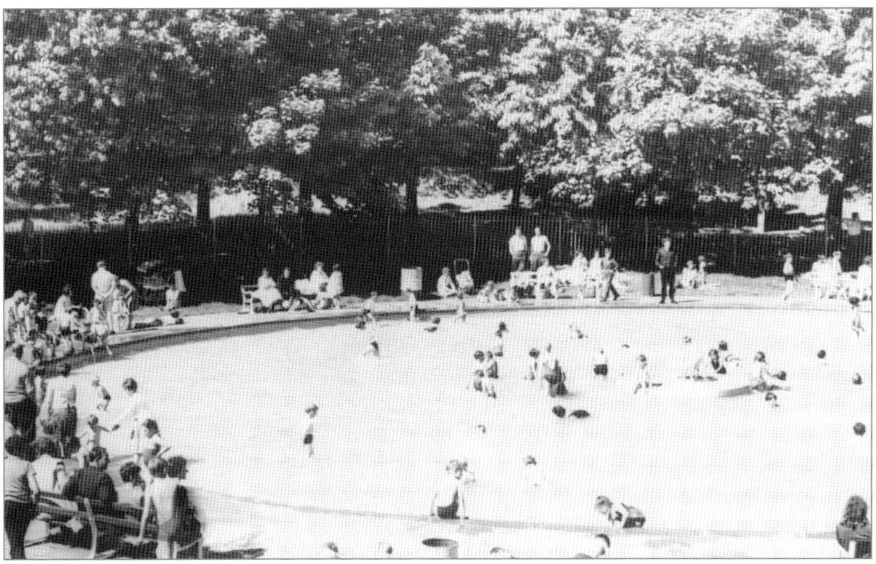

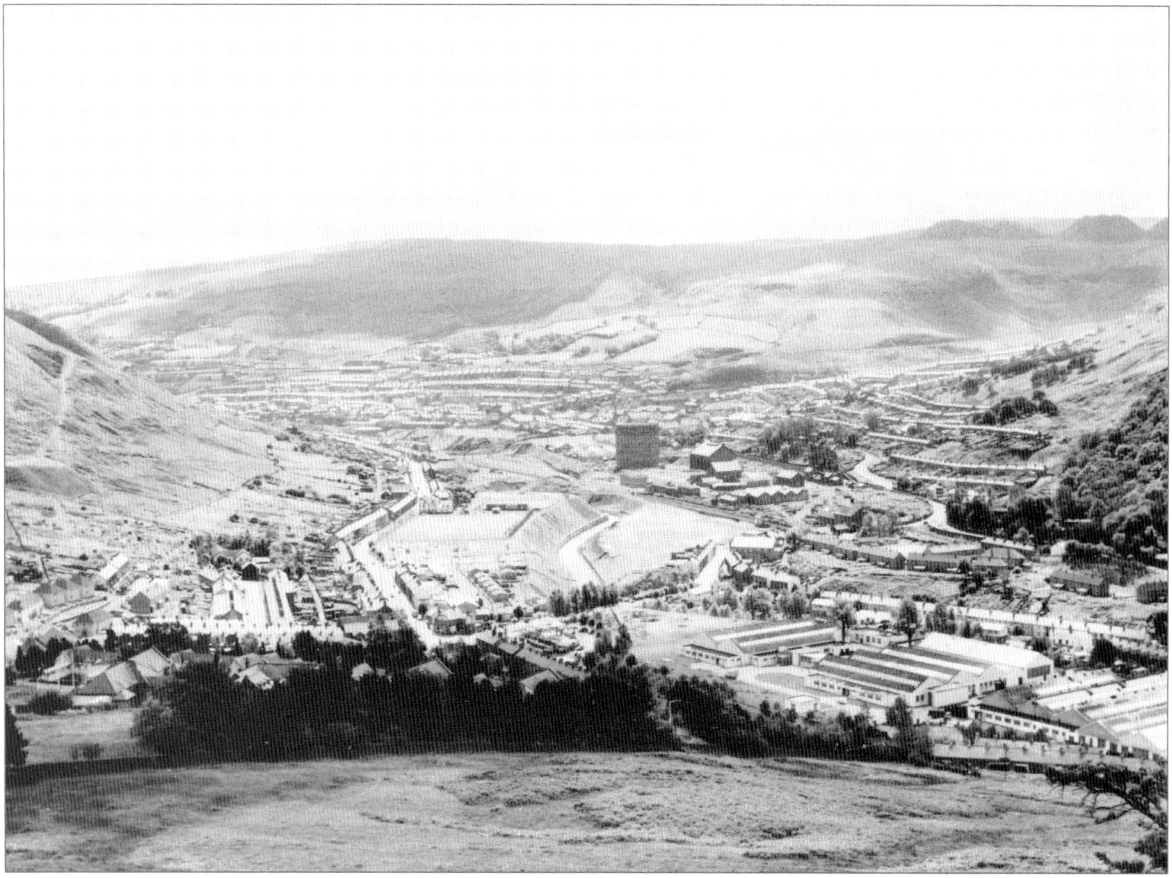

LLWYNYPIA

General View from Mynydd-y-Gelli c1955 L289004

All looks quiet in 1955, as indeed it was, with the end of coal production in 1945. The major pit in this region was the Glamorgan Colliery, known locally as 'The Scotch' after the Scottish miners brought in by the owner, Archibald Hood, in 1862. It remained open for maintenance and pumping until 1966. The colliery also had its own brickworks, and in its heyday produced 10,000 bricks a day made by women in hand moulds, but only the Power House, or Engine House, of the Colliery remains, now a listed building.

LLWYNYPIA
The Square
c1955 L289020

The name Llwynypia means 'the grove of the magpie', and derives from the farm of that name which existed here before the area was industrialised.

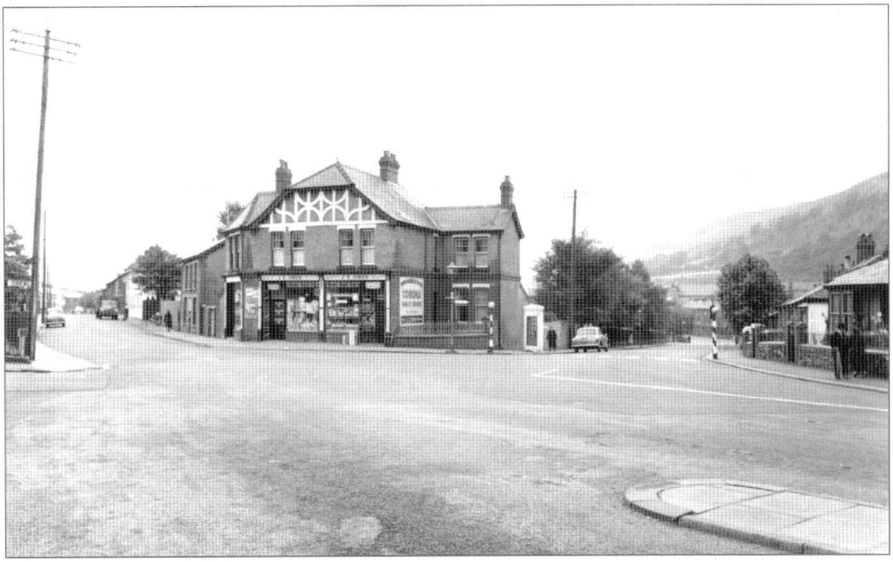

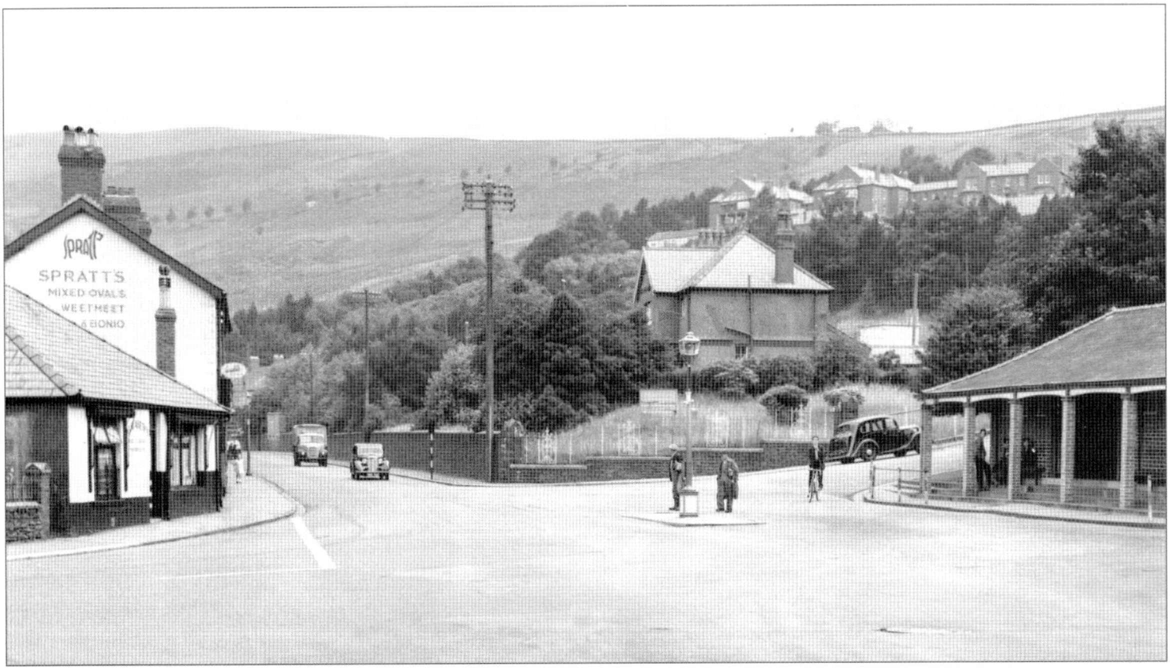

LLWYNYPIA, *General View c1955* L289015

The industrial development of Llwynypia can be mainly attributed to the Scottish mining engineer and entrepreneur Archibald Hood, who came to the Rhondda in 1862. When his company, the Glamorgan Coal Company, became part of the Cambrian Combine in 1908 it was employing thousands of local people. Hood, who died in 1902, was a popular employer, and in 1906 a statue of him was unveiled outside the Llwynypia Miners' Library and Institute, much of the cost for which was raised through donations from his workers.

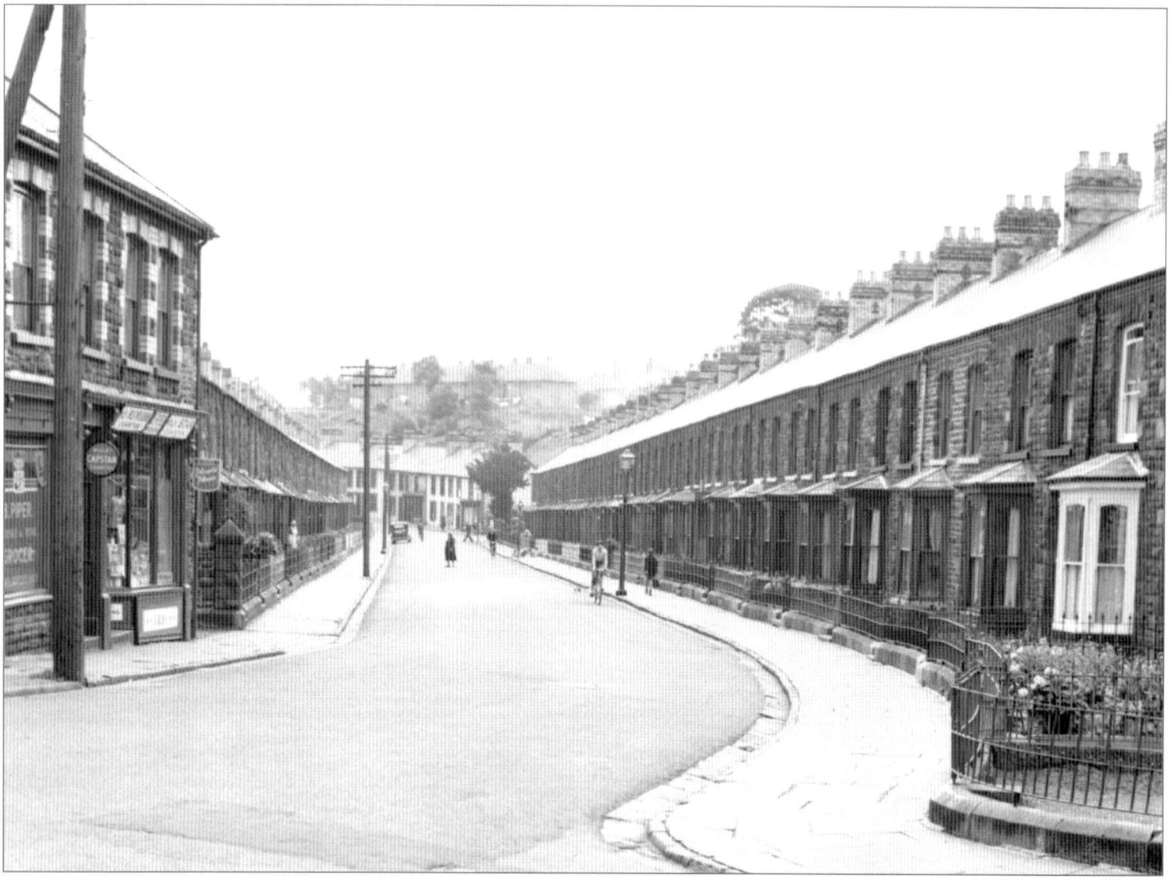

LLWYNYPIA

Sherwood Street c1955 L289013

Sherwood Street in Llwynypia was developed in the late 19th century. It was planned as a high-quality area of attractive houses which would be lived in by owner occupiers, in contrast to the narrow streets of distinctive double-fronted terraced houses known as 'Scotch Terraces' for which Llwynypia is famous. 'Scotch Terraces' were named after the Scottish colliery owner, Archibald Hood, who had them built to house the miners who worked at his nearby Glamorgan Colliery.

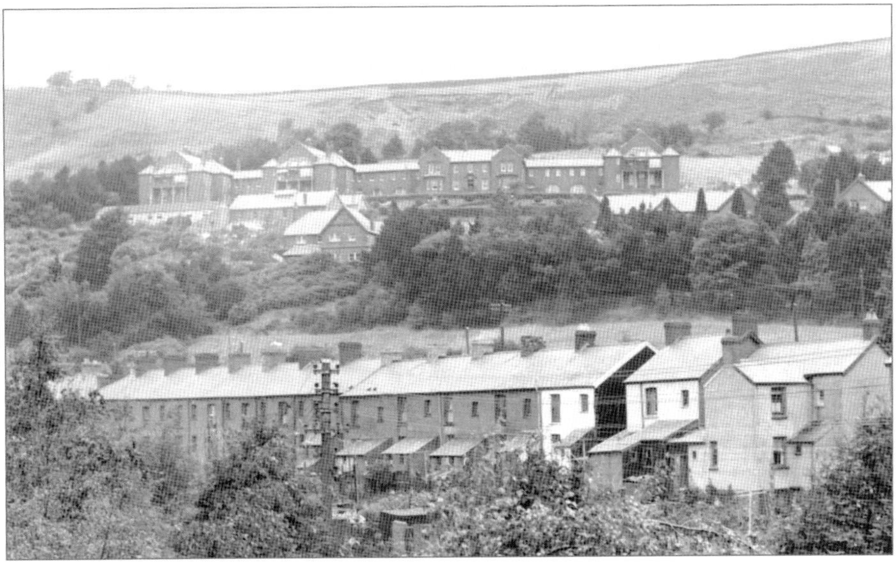

LLWYNYPIA
The Hospital c1955 L289014

Llwynypia Hospital was originally a workhouse, built in 1903 to accommodate the overspill from the Pontypridd establishment. It was known as the Llwynypia Homes. An infirmary was added in 1909, and the complex became Llwynypia Hopsital in 1927. It has since been much extended, and was the first general hospital in the Rhondda.

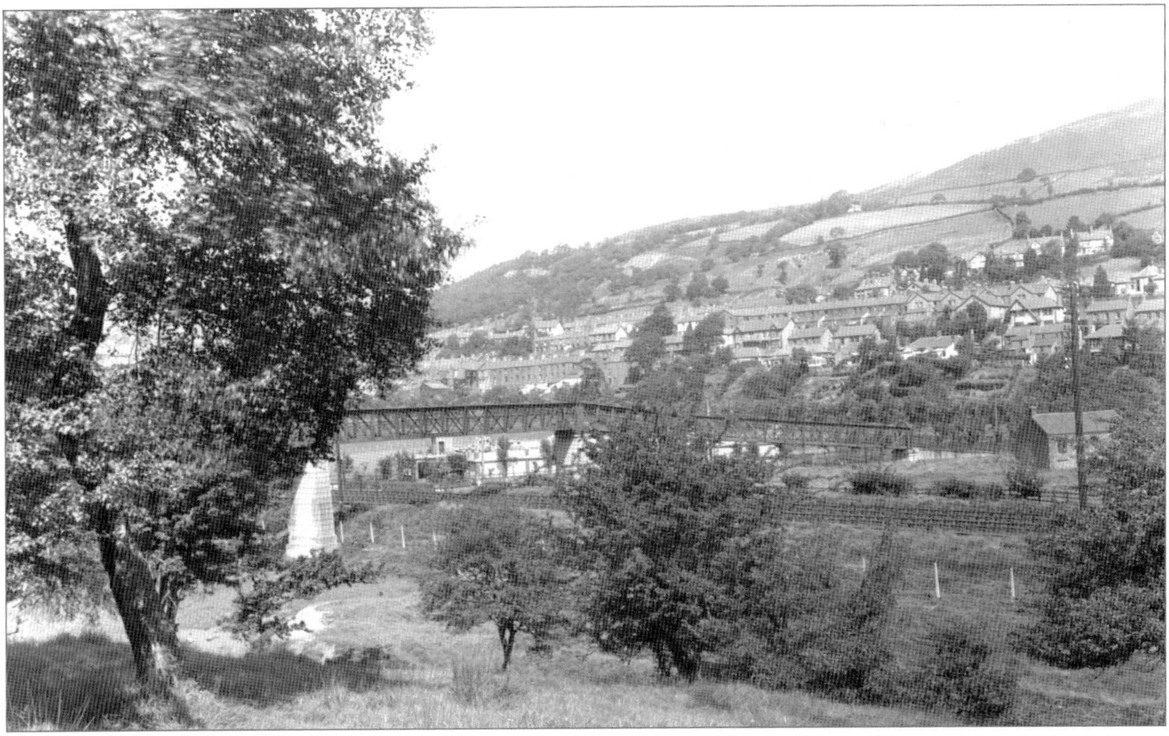

LLWYNYPIA, *From the New Road c1955* L289005

The Llwynypia area was described before industrialisation by the traveller and author Benjamin Heath Malkin (1769-1842) as 'a region of beautiful fields with a magnificent grove at the upper end under the shadow of a towering rock'.

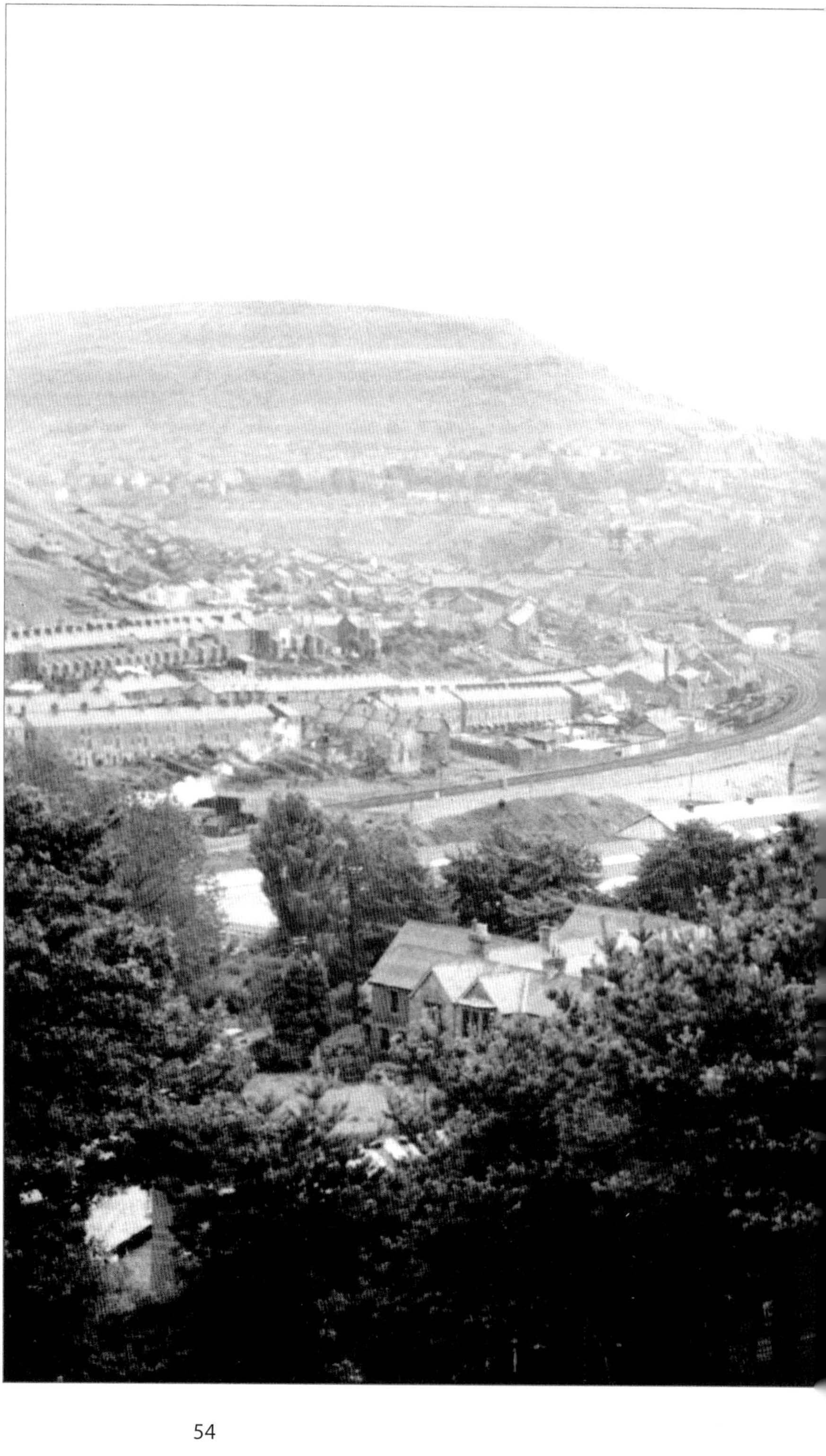

TONYPANDY

General View c1960 T192002

At a glance, the view of Tonypandy seen here is just of another Welsh mining valley, but no book about this area would be complete without a mention of the 'Tonypandy Riots' of 1910, which originated in a lock-out of workers employed at the Cambrian Combine's Ely Pit in Penygraig. Events escalated into a widespread strike thoughtout the area, and hundreds of police were sent in to keep order. Following the death of a miner the strike became a full-blown riot and instead of negotiations, the Home Secretary, Winston Churchill, followed up by ordering the army in. This was enough to light the touchpaper and it also did much to make Churchill's name anathema in the Valleys. The very act of using the soldiers also led to a great distrust of the Government in London and hastened the rapid rise of Socialism and the Labour Party in South Wales.

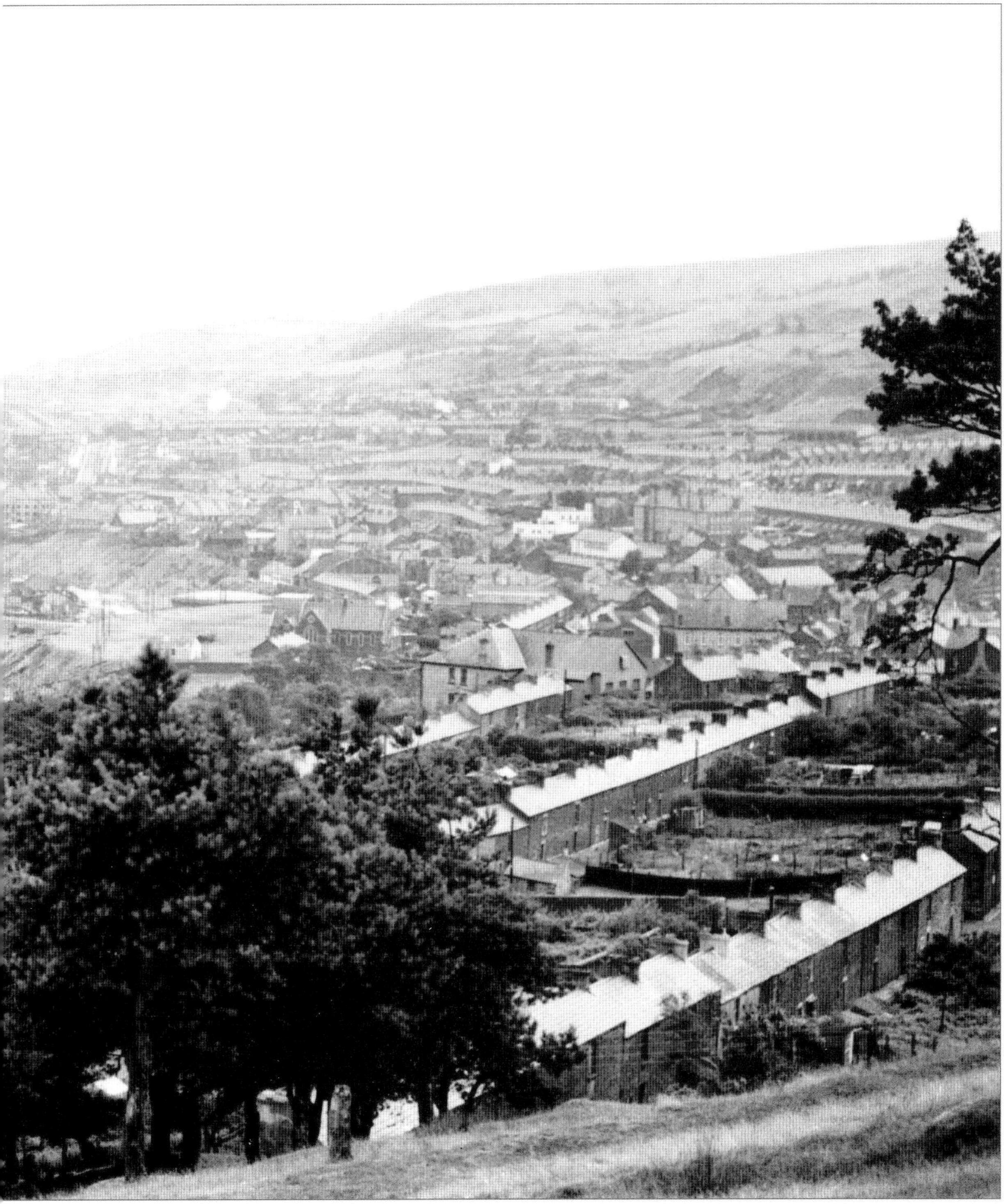

TREALAW
Brithweunydd Road c1965
T193008

A well-kept, neat street running out of Trealaw centre, with all the accoutrements of modern living. The shops are congregated round the telephone box in the distance, whilst on the right, next to the fish and chip shop a lady sweeps her step. There are more TV aerials on the right than on the left indicating the vagaries of TV reception in a low valley.

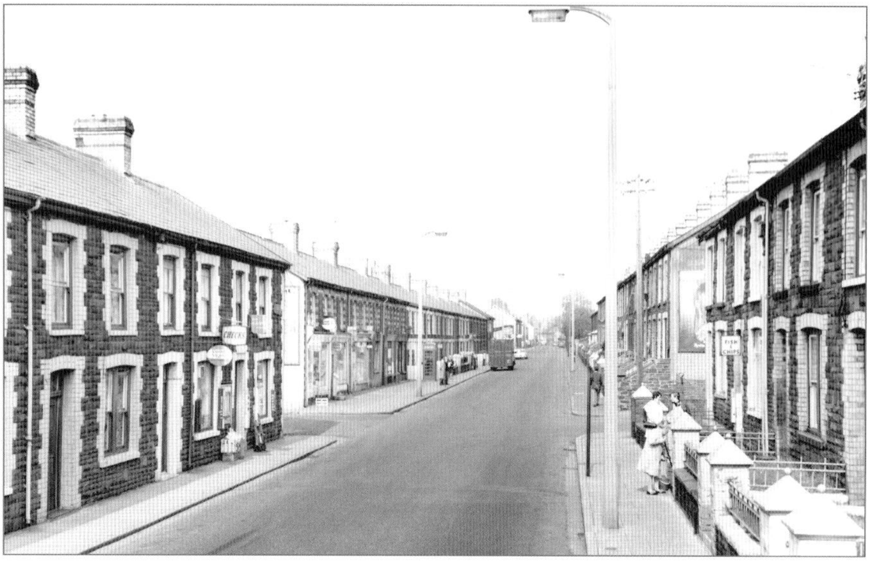

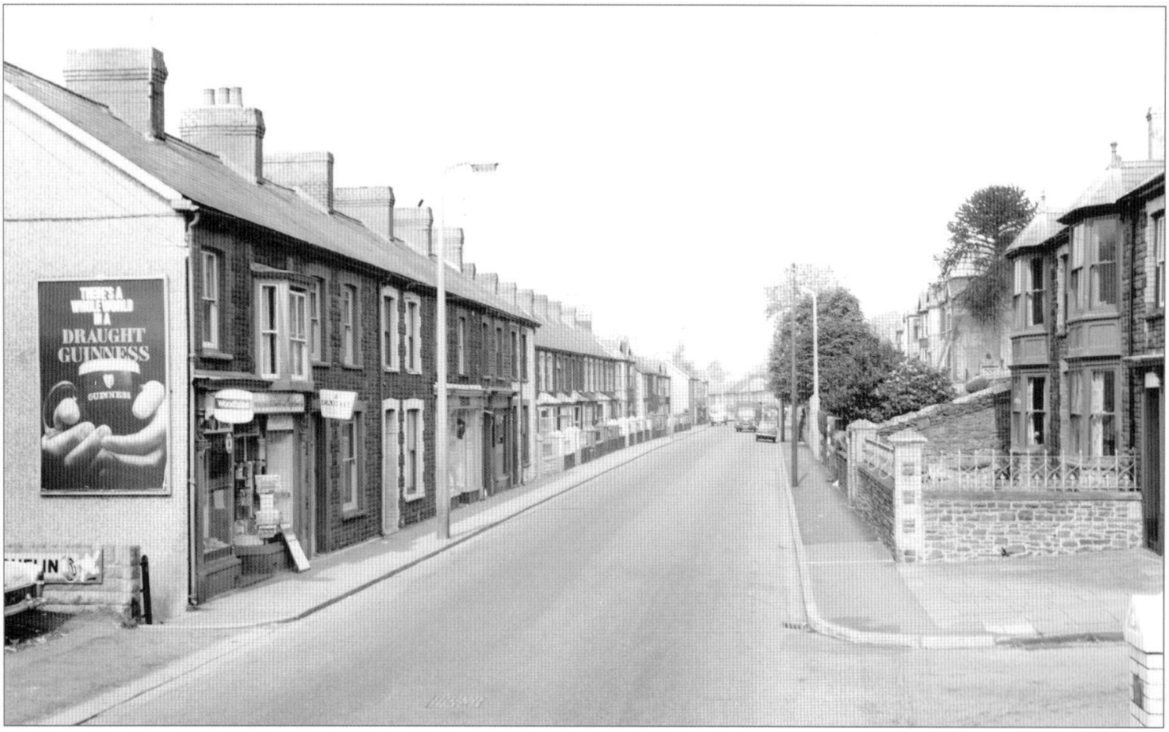

TREALAW, *Brithweunydd Road c1965* T193010

The shop on the left of this view displays posters and signs advocating the 'benefits' of 'Guinness' plus 'Woodbines', 'Cadets' and also 'jars of sweets'. A healthy diet indeed.

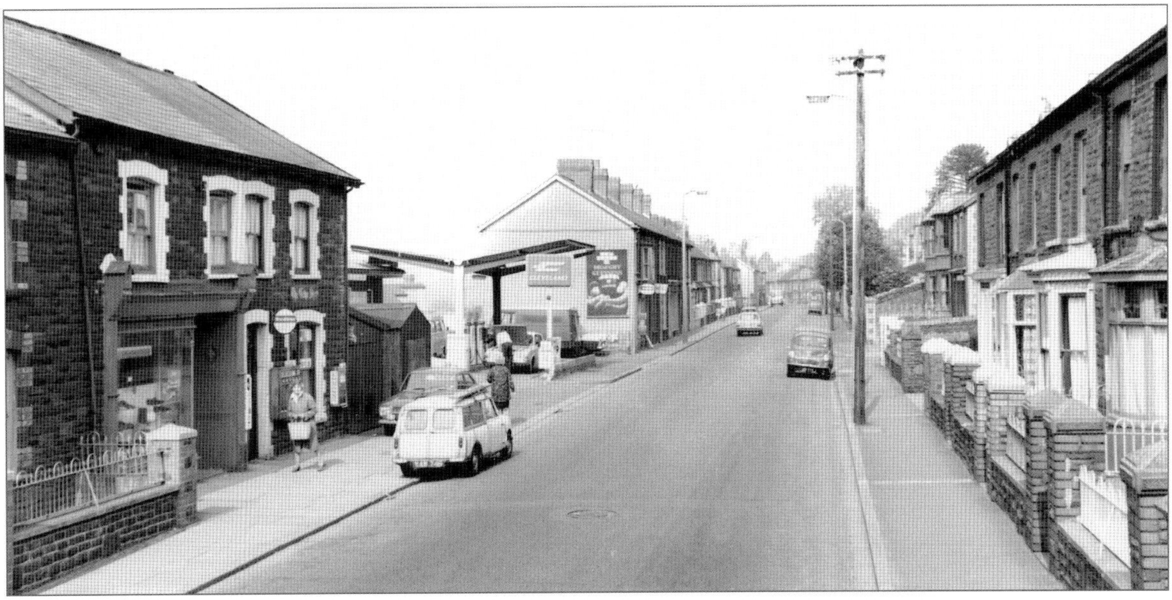

TREALAW, *Brithweunydd Road c1965* T193009

This shows the same street but in a longer shot so that the 'Cleveland' filling station is now visible with a customer checking under the bonnet. The contrasted white windows and doorways is an agreeable feature but by looking at the last three pictures it is not everywhere, more of a random feature. And if the shop was closed there was a handy vending machine on the outside wall.

TREALAW, *Cemetery Road c1965*
T193007a

The premises in this photograph now houses the Trealaw Workingmen's Club; sited opposite the local cemetery, it has been nicknamed 'The Res', or 'Resurrection Club'.

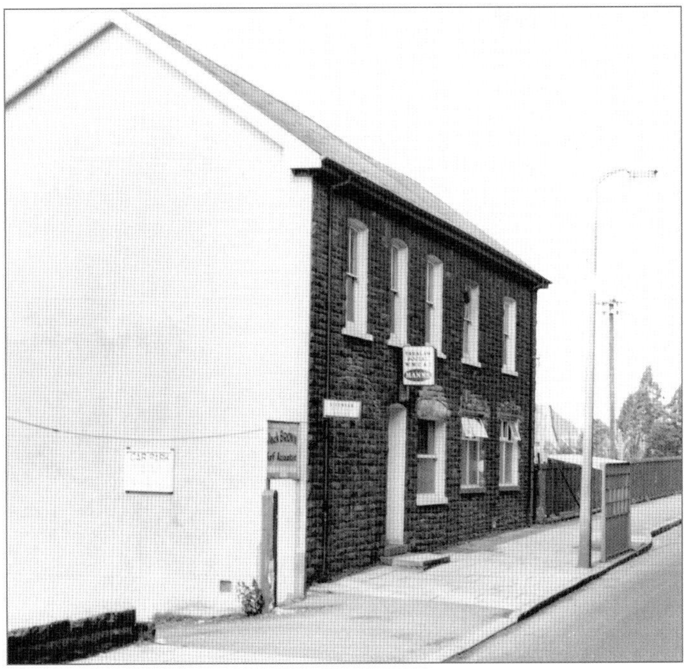

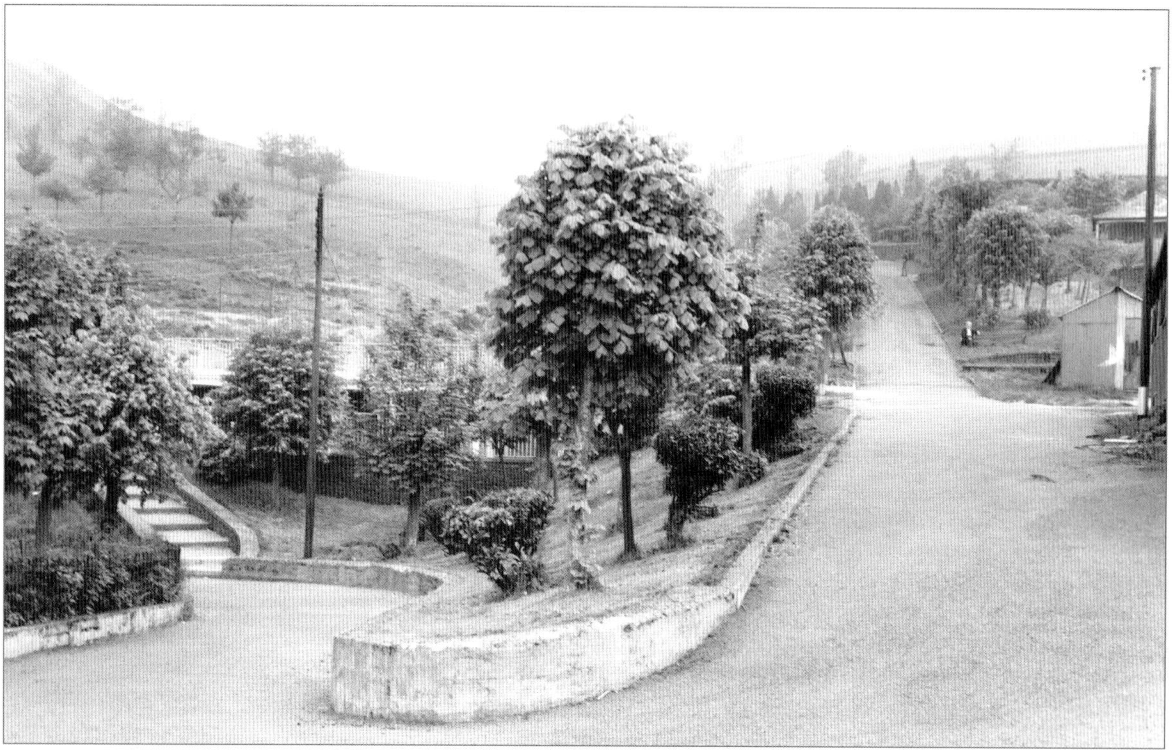

TREALAW
Garth Park c1965 T193004

The Park at Trealaw was planned and built in the 1930s by local unemployed miners during the Depression. At one time Garth Park offered facilities for swimming, bowls, tennis and football, but in later years it was allowed to become derelict and overgrown, as seen in the photographs on these pages.

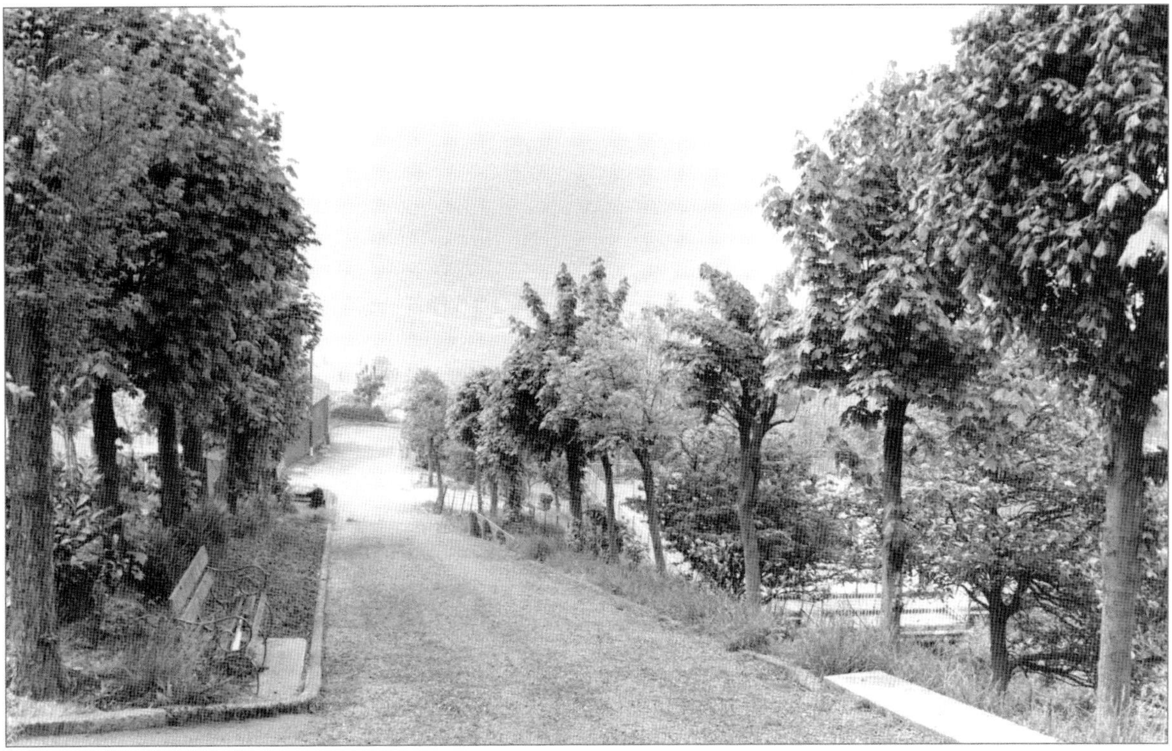

▲ **TREALAW,** *Garth Park c1965* T193003

This shot exemplifies the state of the park at this time. It is in a bad state of neglect, the trees need trimming back, the roadway deserves better than rough gravel. Even the bench doesn't look safe to sit on.

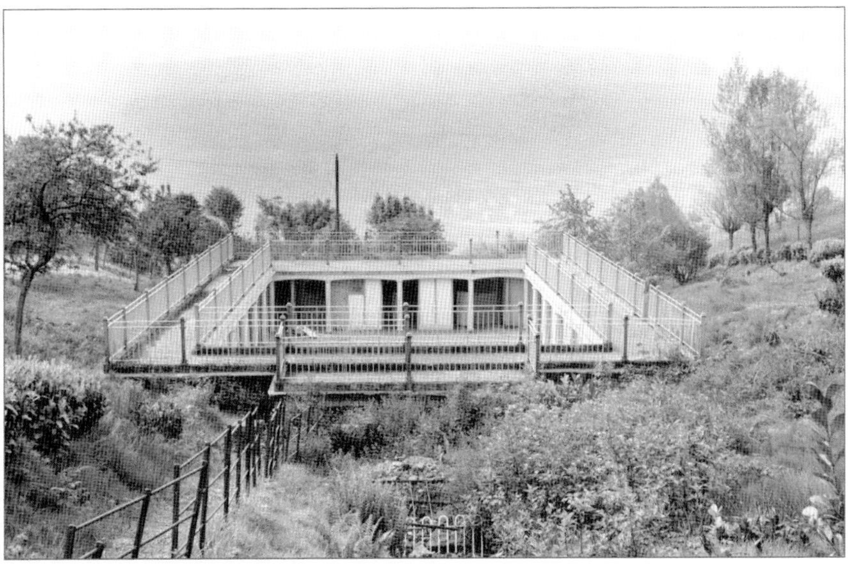

◄ **TREALAW**
Garth Park c1965 T193001

Garth Park's once grand full-size swimming pool, long-since empty and in a state of total disrepair, is seen here. The fences are collapsing and the undergrowth is encroaching on all sides.

PENYGRAIG
Tylacelyn Road c1955 P221006

This road is the main thoroughfare through the town and as usual, before the coming of the omnipotent supermarket, there was a shop or trader for everything. Top left is the 'District Pharmacy' and opposite are the modern frontages of the 'co-op' and haberdashery.

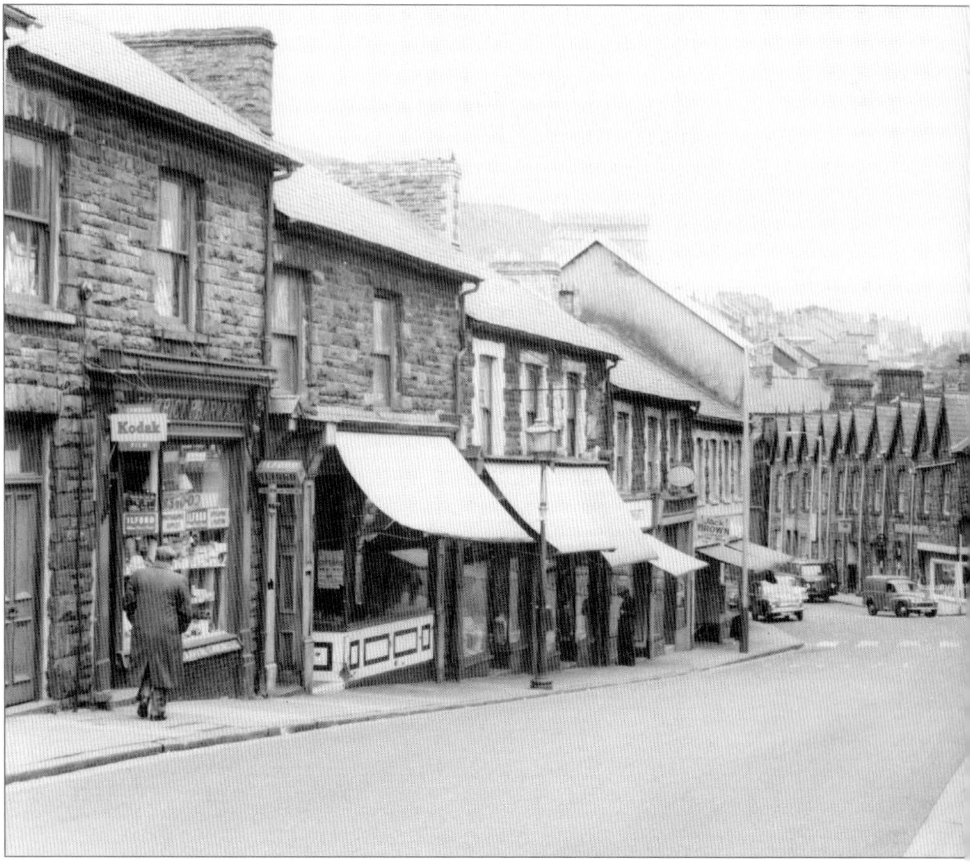

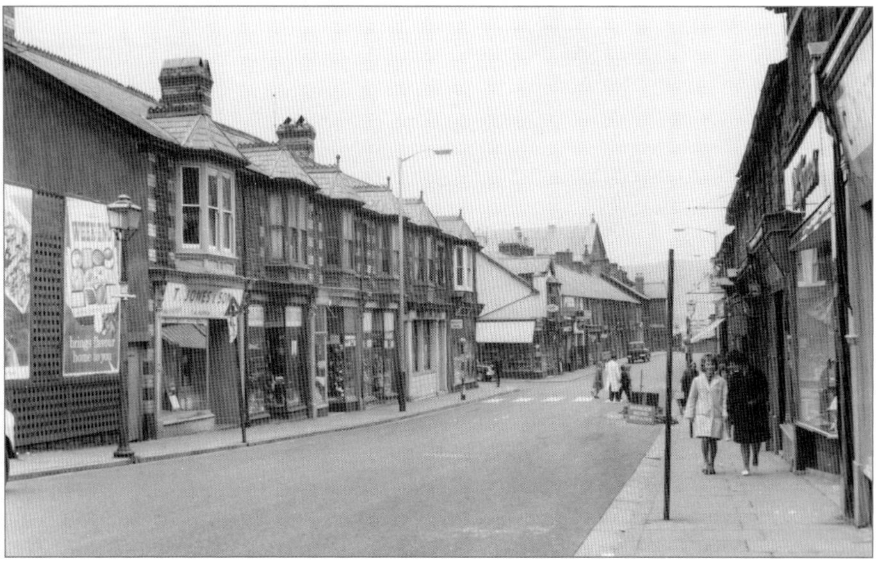

PENYGRAIG
Tylacelyn Road c1955
P221007

Further down the street the shops here have gained the feature of an upper bay window. Road repairs of a minor nature are being undertaken just before the crossing patrol, or 'lollipop man'. The street lighting by now is electrical but there is a nice relic from times past in the shape of a gaslight, just before 'Mr Jones' Newsagency'.

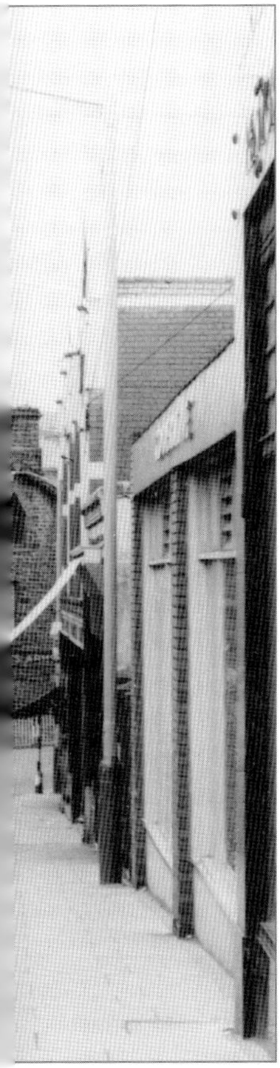

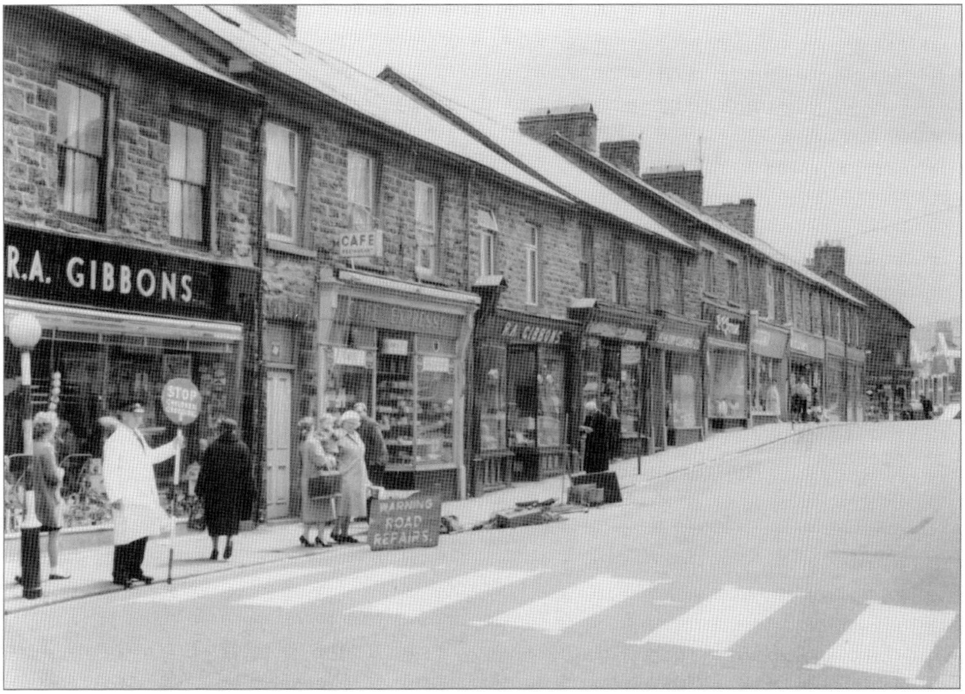

▲ **PENYGRAIG,** *Tylacelyn Road c1955* P221008

This picture follows on from the last but it was taken from the other side of the roadworks with the ever-vigilant 'lollipop man' guarding his post with only one lone cyclist approaching. Mr Gibbons was a man of some standing, having two shops.

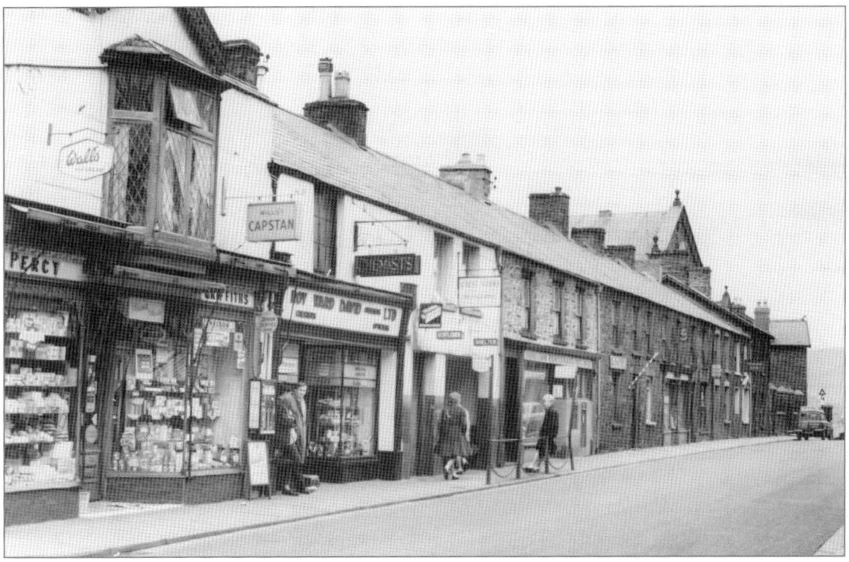

◄ **PENYGRAIG**
Tylacelyn Road c1955
P221009

Here you could do everything; shop at 'Percys' then visit the toilets by the bus stop - but only if you were a 'Gentleman', the other sign being 'Shelter'. Proceed for a haircut where the barber's pole protrudes, pick up a copy of the 'Sport Echo' from the van before paying-in to the last building, the Midland Bank.

PENYGRAIG
Tylacelyn Road 1963
P221010

This section of the road seems to be more drab, or at least the shops and buildings do. The lighter touch comes from the three girls in identical dress, by the crossing sign on the left. One cannot help but ponder - Waitresses? Bank Tellers? Hairdressers? Or simply shop workers?

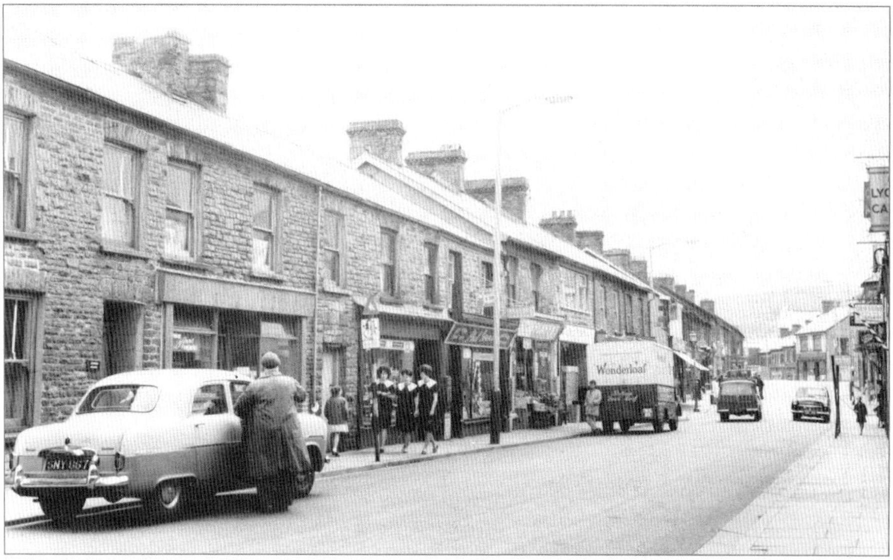

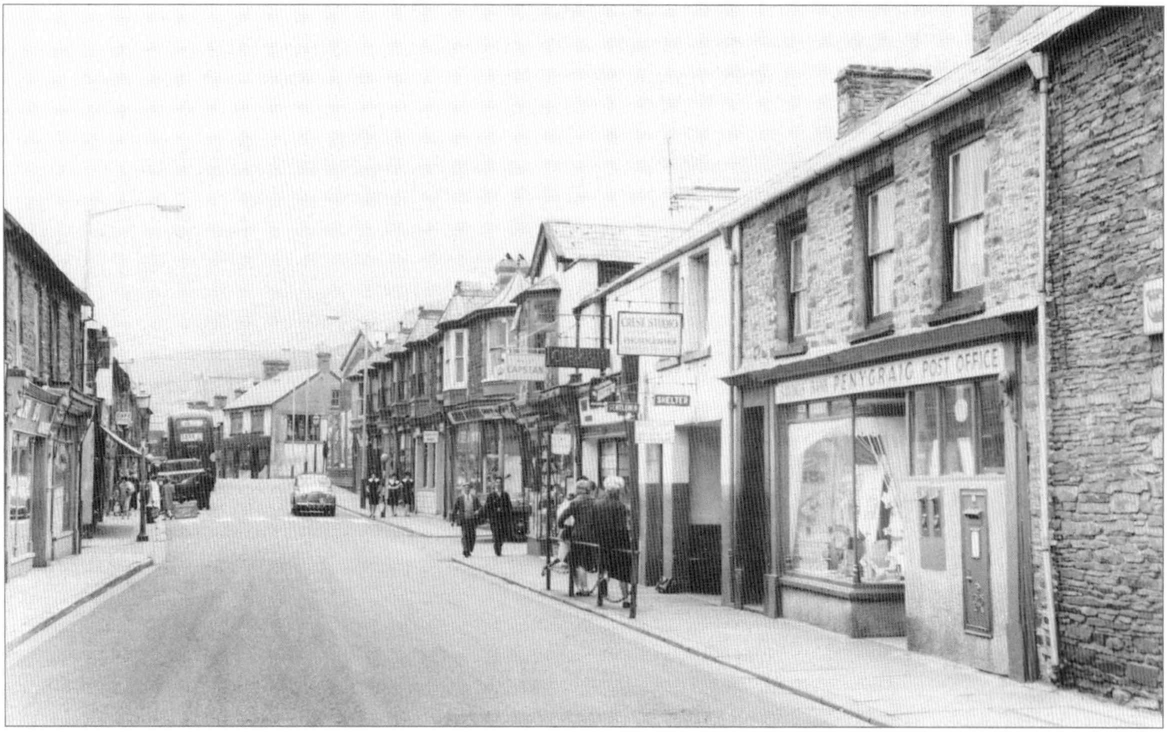

PENYGRAIG, *Tylacelyn Road c1955* P221011

The name of the original settlement in this area was recorded on a map in the mid-19th century as 'Ffrwd Amos', and this early name is recalled in the name of Amos Hill. The name Penygraig derives from the name of the first mine in the area.

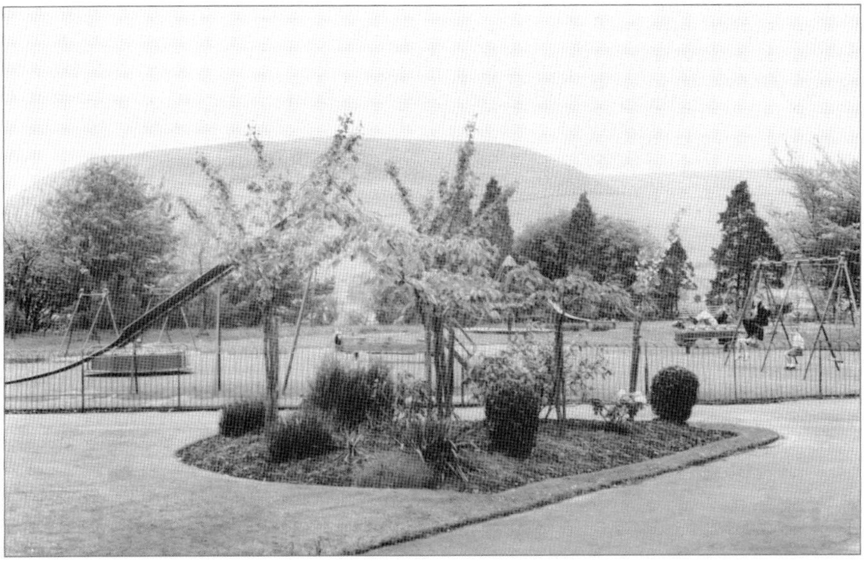

PENYGRAIG
The Park, The Children's Recreation Ground c1955
P221003

The town was not a big mining area so in addition to one well-stocked main street there is really only the park in which to relax. Most of the towns in the Rhondda towns all had sizeable parks out of proportion to the population. But with the exhausting working week the miners and their families needed to get away, if only for a Sunday. The children's area here has everything for some fun, including the wooden 'rocking horse'.

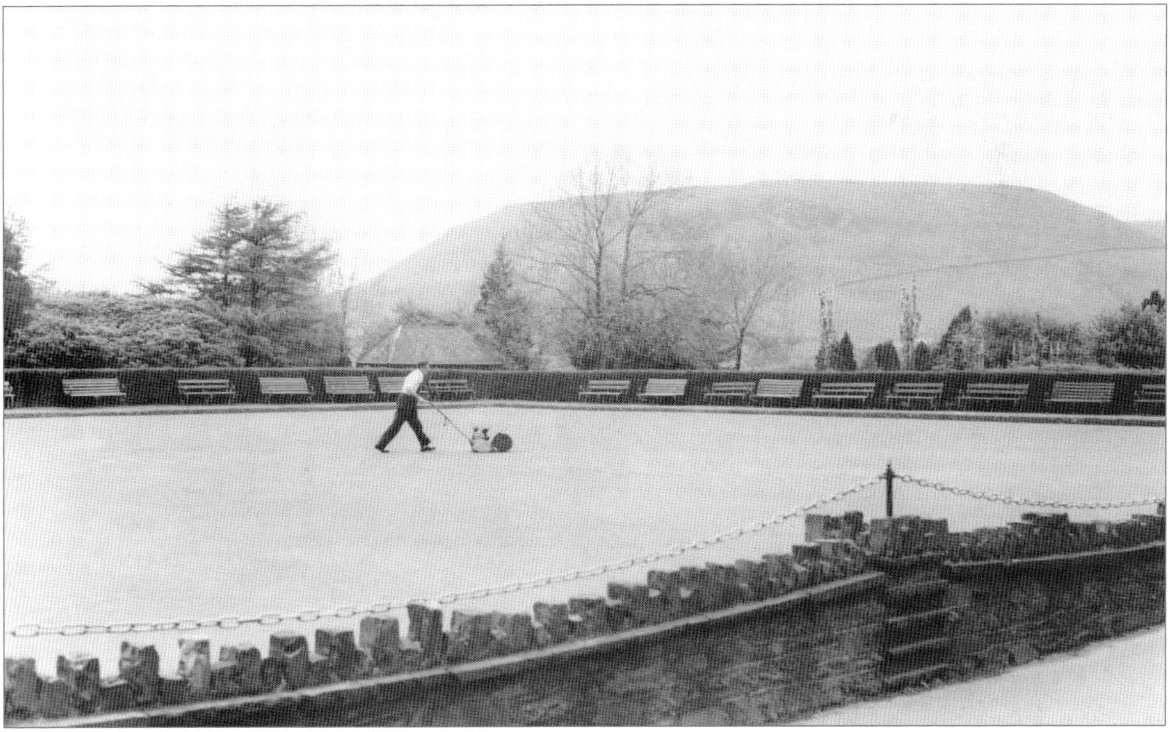

PENYGRAIG, *The Bowling Green c1955* P221002

Striding out to keep the grass perfect for a game of 'woods' is the groundsman and he appears to be doing a fine job. The spectators' wooden benches are innumerable and the whole is enclosed within an ornamental wall surmounted by chain. All in all the Bowling Green contrasts sharply with the barren mountains in the background.

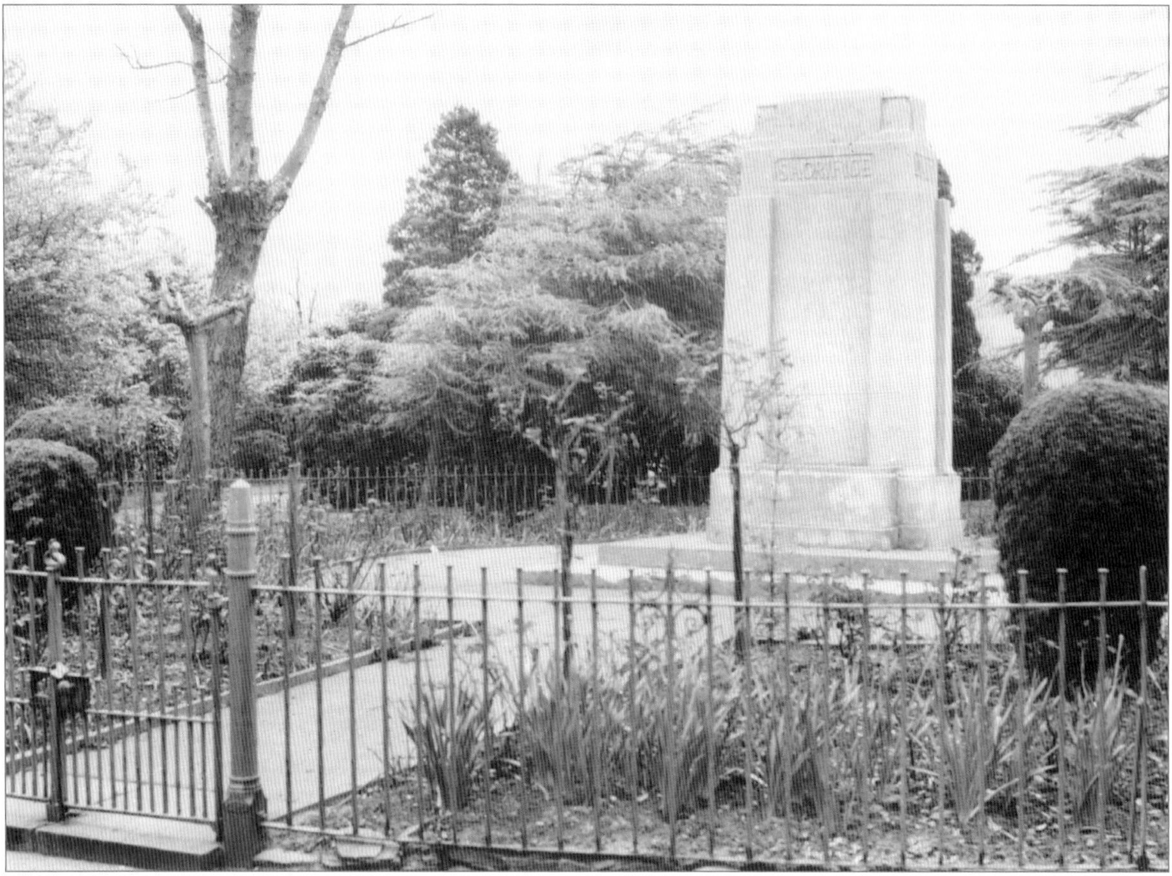

PENYGRAIG

The Park, The Memorial c1955 P221001

An elegant fence and gate lead into the enclosure that houses the War Memorial. Within the grounds the flowerbeds are well tended and the privet-like bushes are regularly and neatly trimmed. The Memorial itself appears to break with tradition (on this side at least) by not listing those killed in action. Instead it has the one evocative word, 'Sacrifice'.

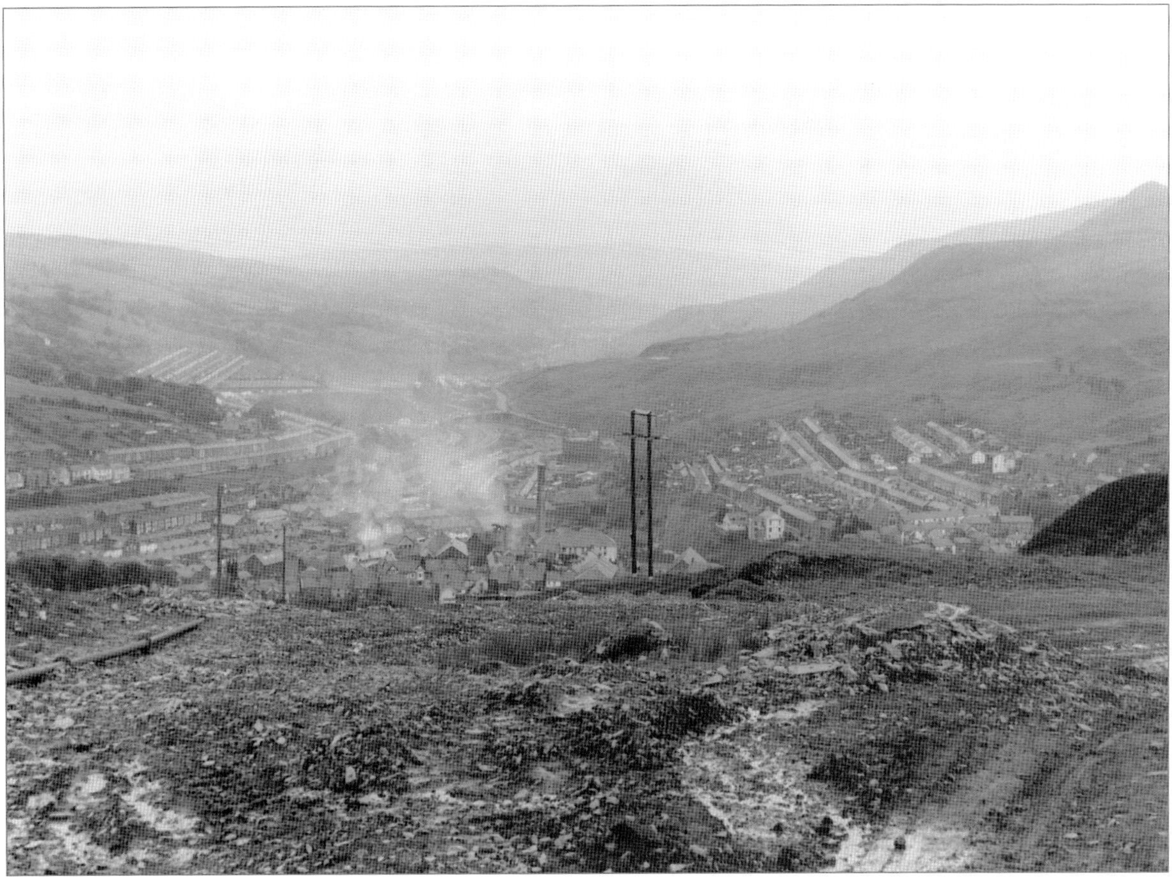

PORTH

Mount Pleasant c1960 P280020

As a memento to the worst degradation of the coal-mining century, and to the Industrial Revolution in general, this awful scene of the leftover debris is as bad as it gets. The whole foreground is just scree, slag and filth. Even the pit workings themselves are obscured by the ashen smog.

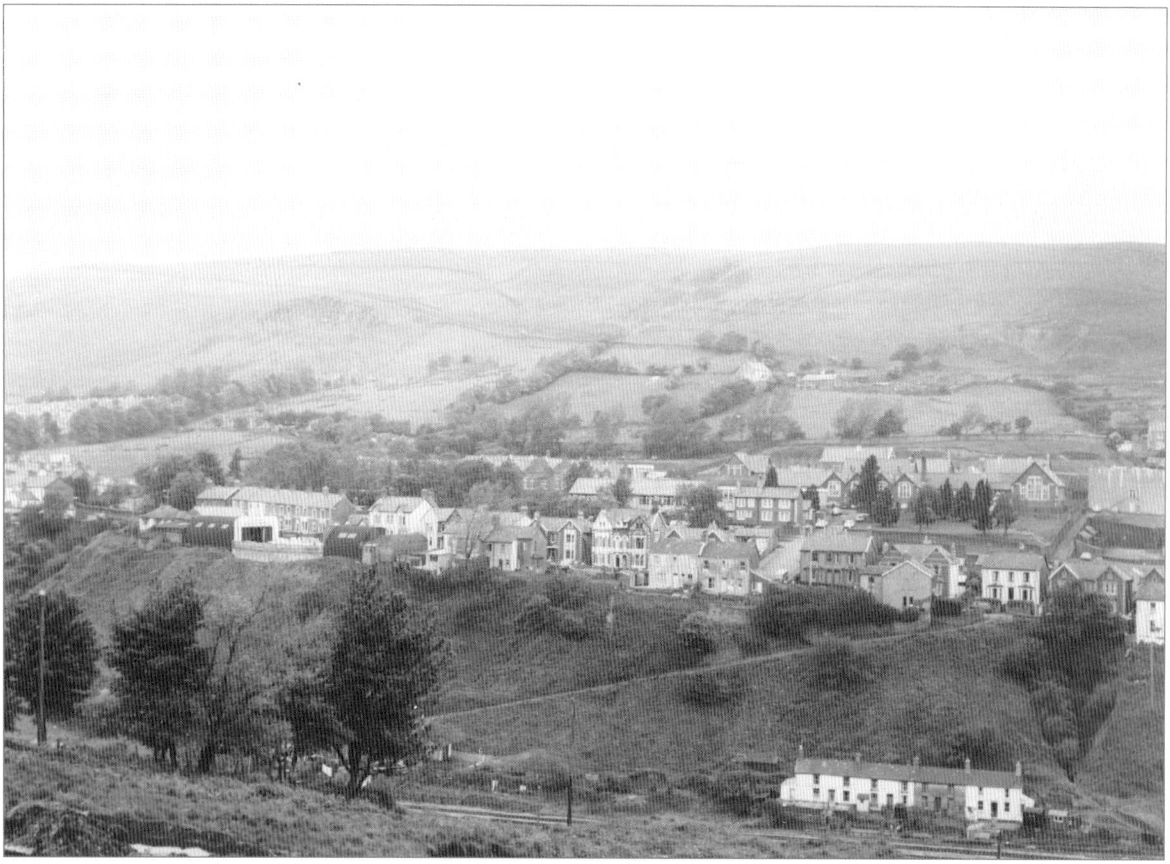

PORTH

General View c1955 P280003

The meaning of 'Porth' in English is 'gateway', and this town is the dividing point of the two valleys of the Rhondda and the confluence of the two rivers at the southernmost point of the region. A famous name in Porth's history is that of Thomas & Evans, the company which produced the 'Corona' soft drinks. The founding director of the company, Thomas Evans, gave Bronwydd Park to Rhondda District Council in 1921, and a bronze bust of him can be seen in the park.

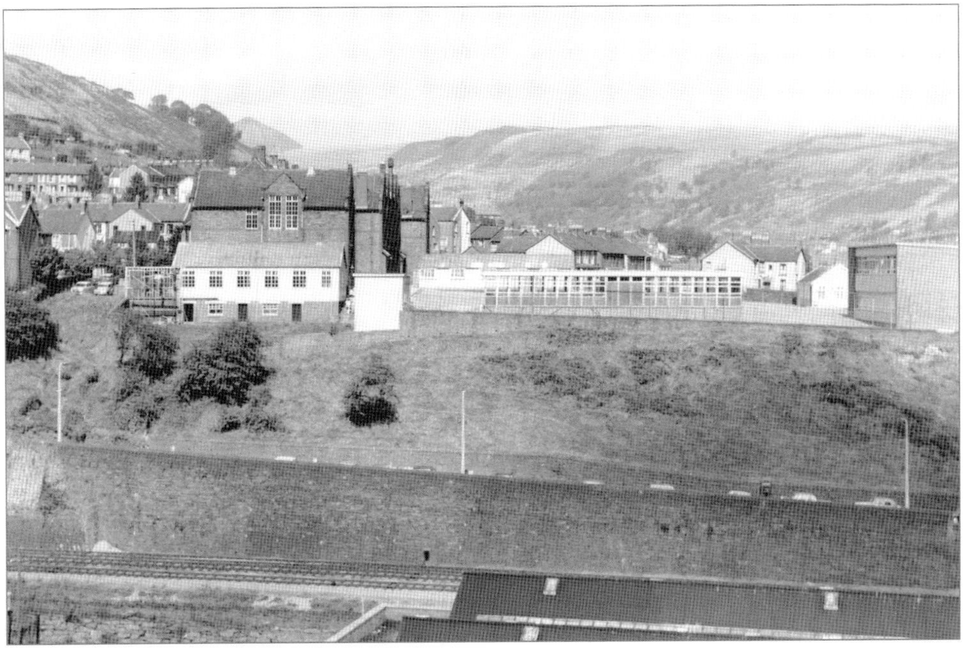

PORTH
The Grammar School c1955
P280008

Above the railway and then the main road the principal feature here is the old Grammar School. Not much of the main school building is shown other than the gable end but leading off to the left is an additioonal 'temporary' classroom. This leads down to the sports hall and gymnasium.

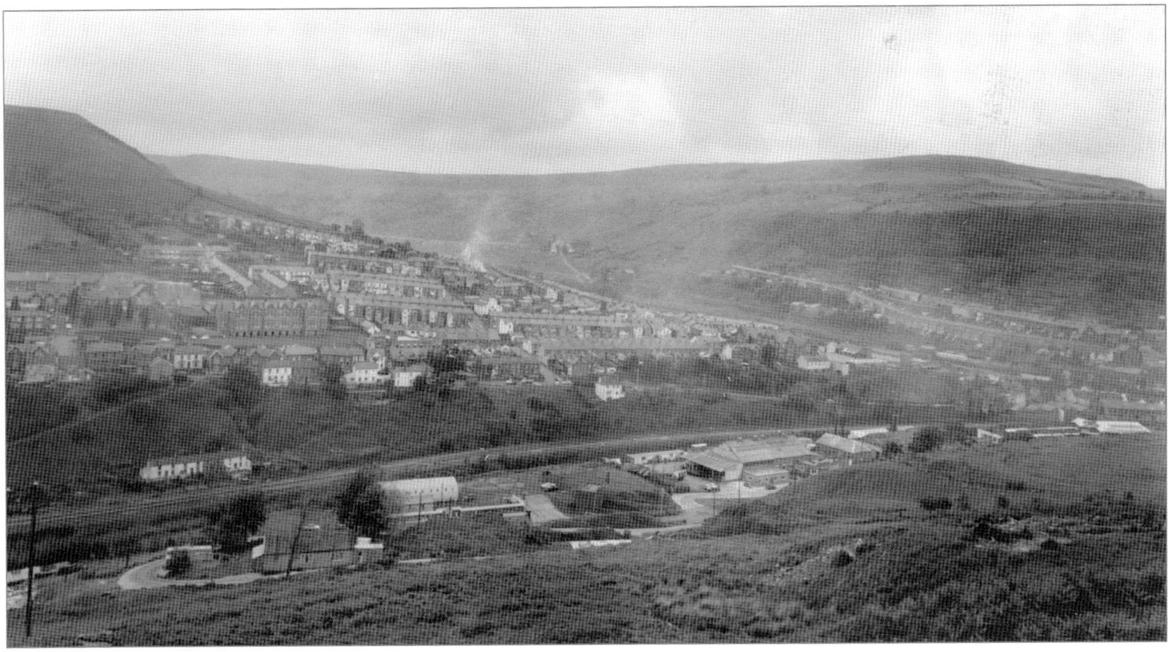

PORTH, *Mount Pleasant c1960* P280019

The panorama here continues from a previous photograph with the terrace of cottages seen again alongside the railway track that runs right across the bottom of both photographs. The view is so typical of a Rhondda township, with its barren landscape and the dwellings built as high as possible.

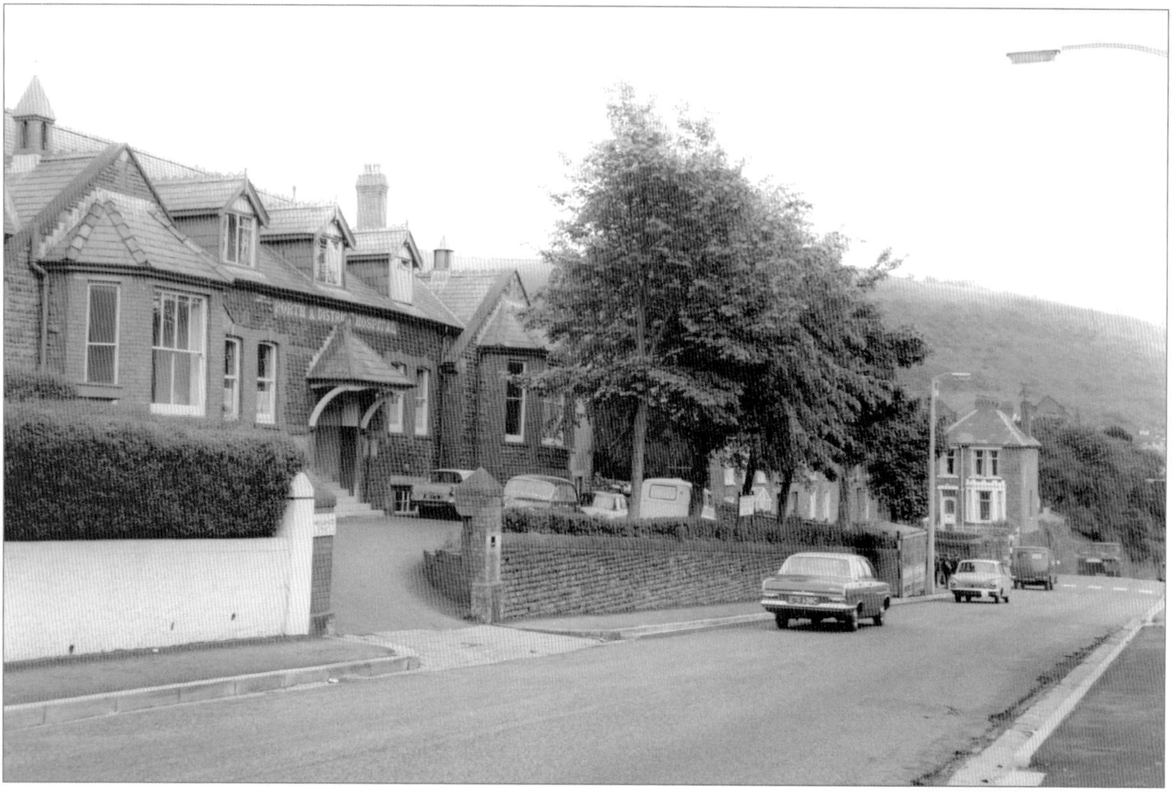

PORTH

Cottage Hospital c1955 P280001

The 'cottage hospital' was originally a small facility with few or no resident medical staff, more akin to a nursing home in today's language. However, the sign above the doorway says 'Porth and District Hospital', so by the time of the photograph it may well have been offering wider medical services. It is a pleasing, if somewhat fussy, building with large bays and three symmetrical dormers. Hopefully the fact that it is situated on Cemetery Road has no reflection on the standard of care.

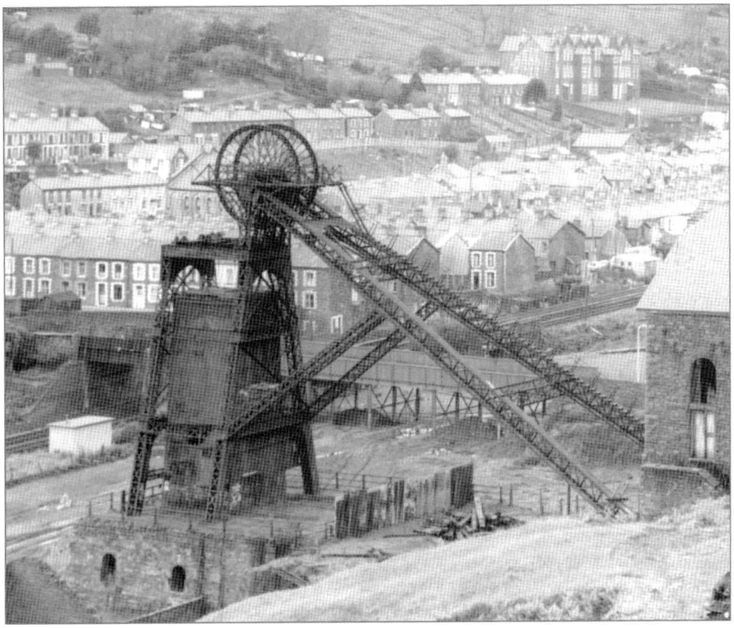

YNYSHIR
The Pit c1965 Y33001a

We now move up the valley of the Rhondda Fach, and come to Ynyshir. The immense size of the winding house and gear in this photograph dwarfs the tiny cottages in the background.

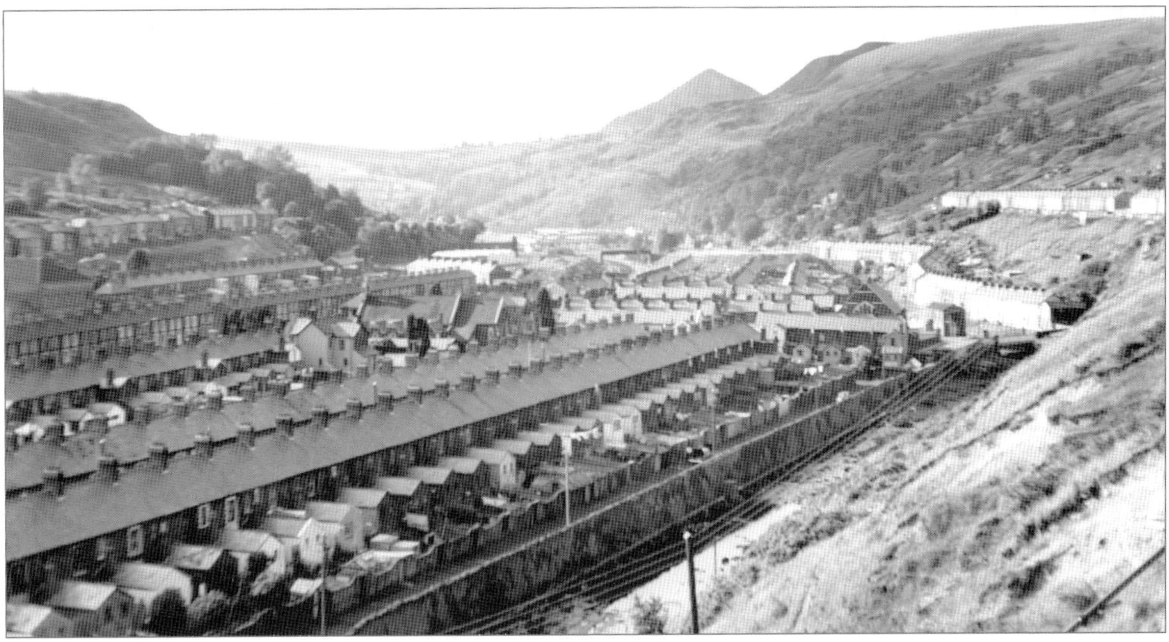

YNYSHIR, *General View c1965* Y33002

This is an excellent photograph of a Rhondda pit village and shows how it was necessary to build the terraced houses in a string along the valley bottom. Hemmed in by the mountains it was the only way to go and the reason why so many towns in the area almost meet. This in turn makes it difficult for the stranger to know exactly which 'pit town' he may be in.

YNYSHIR, *The Park c1965* Y33006

As we have seen even the smallest colliery village wherever it may be in the Rhondda Valleys has its own park. This one looks more suited to the youngsters of the area with its swings and slide. The pit engine house and shaft is now in the distance.

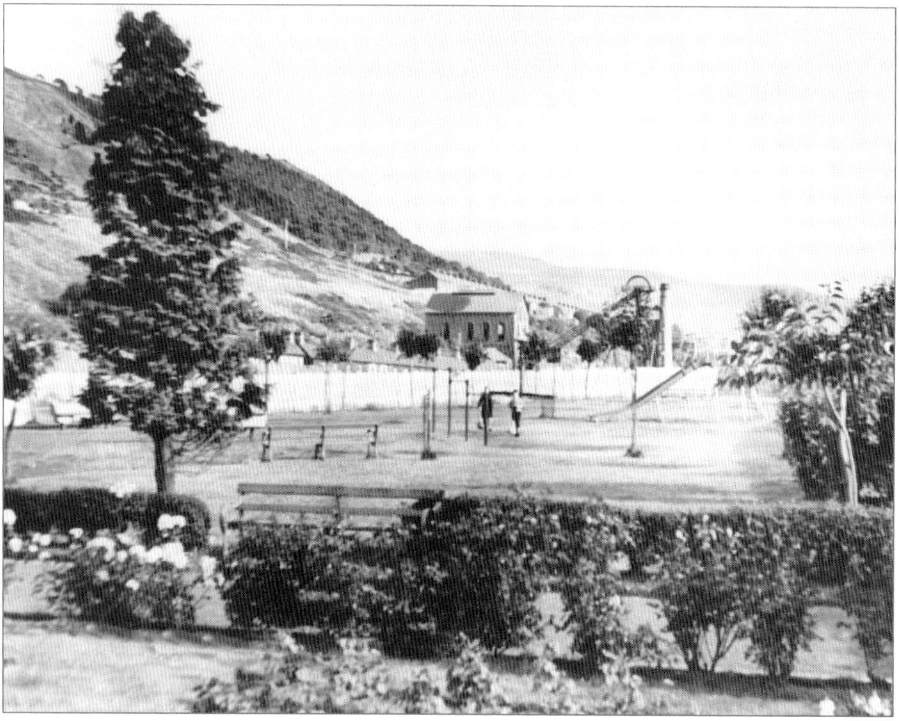

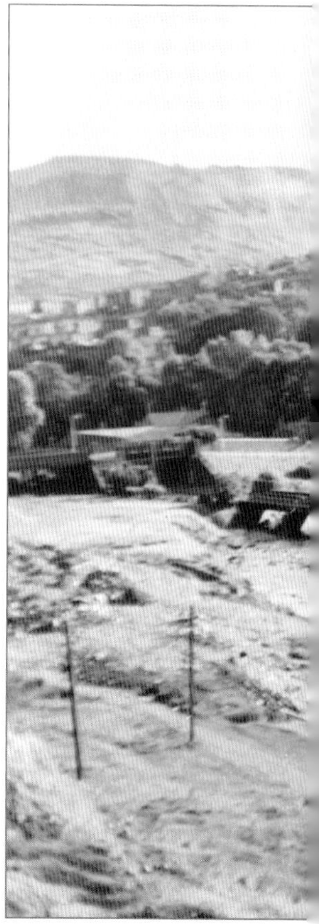

YNYSHIR
c1965 Y33010

The steep and narrow lane leads the eye down to a more agreeable view of the town. It also gives us more of a feeling of the topography of the region and again shows how the valleys are recovering their health after the years of grimy air. Grass grows on this side while the forests reclaim the hillside across the valley.

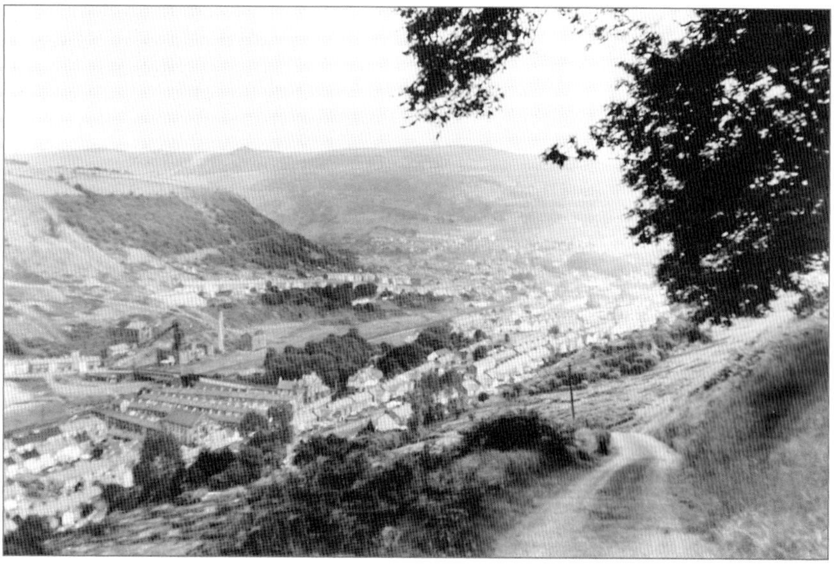

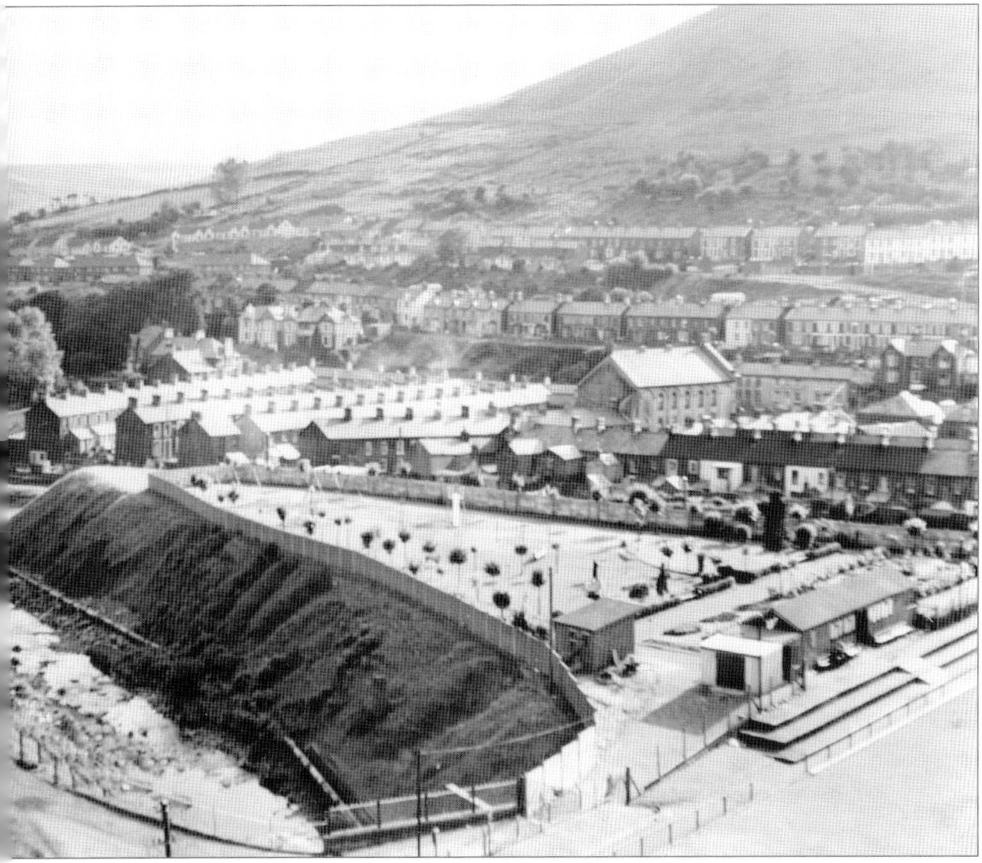

YNYSHIR
General View c1965
Y33003

This may be a typical view but the principal feature is the slagheap, which has been walled off and re-surfaced with asphalt to create a leisure and play area. The lesson seems to be, 'If it's there, don't try to hide it, but use it for better things'

YNYSHIR
Heath Terrace c1965
Y33004

A motor cycle and sidecar has pulled off the road and their owners do indeed seem to be admiring the view. In the far distance the conical shape of a large slagheap can be seen.

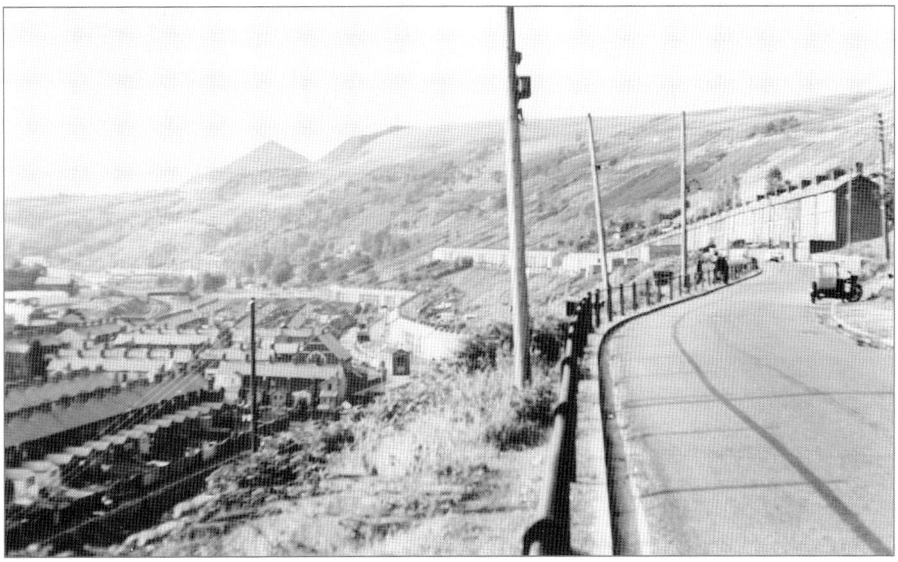

FERNDALE *and Blaenllechau c1955* F123002

After coalmining became established here in the 1860s, Ferndale became the main township of the Rhondda Fach. The first miners here and their families were housed in wooden huts, known as 'the barracks', which a reporter from The Times in 1867 described as 'houses rudely built of wood, like American log huts'.

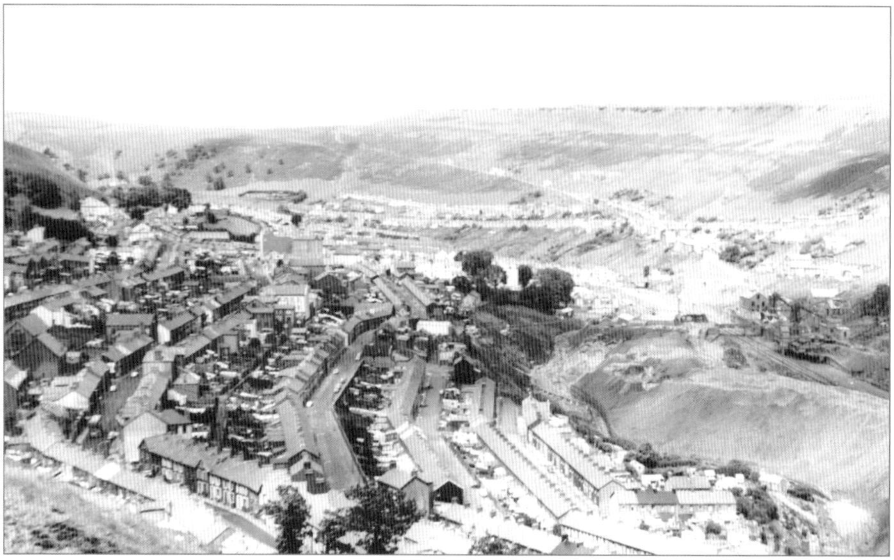

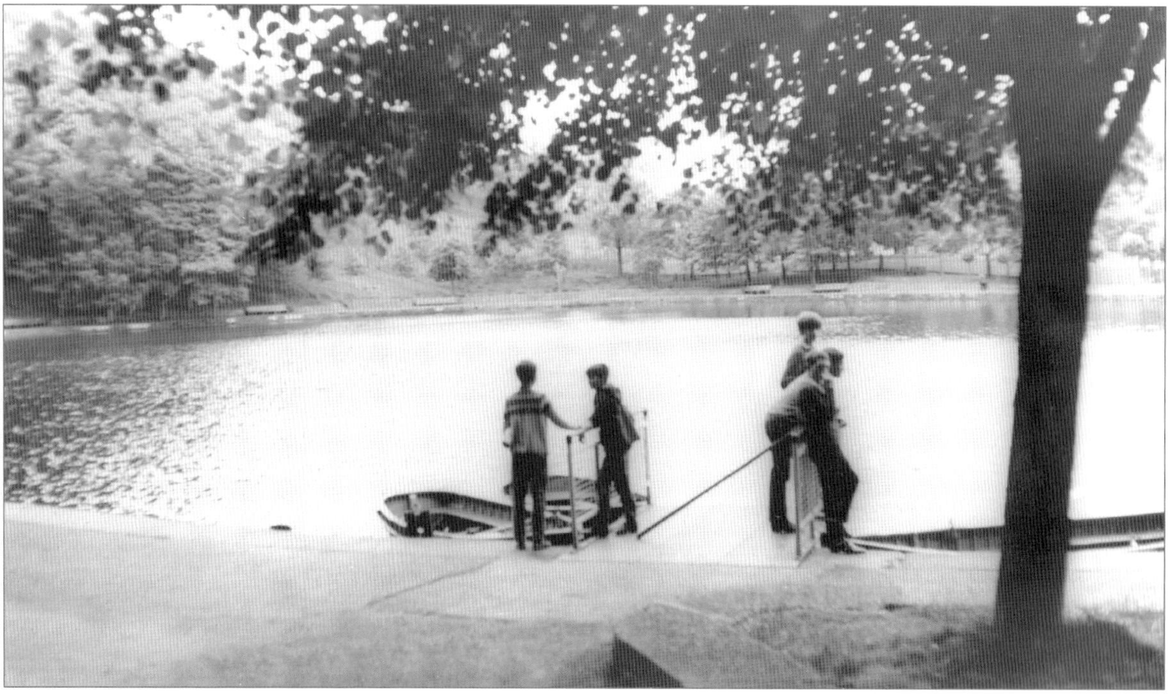

FERNDALE, *Darran Park Lake c1955* F123007

The lake in Darran Park is known as 'Llyn y Forwyn', or 'The Maiden's Lake'. The legend says that a young man called Gwyn once married a beautiful maiden called Nelferch, who rose from the waters of the lake to meet him. Nelferch warned Gwyn that she would leave him if they quarrelled three times, and, in time, that is exactly what happened. Nelferch went back to live beneath the water of the lake, and was never seen again.

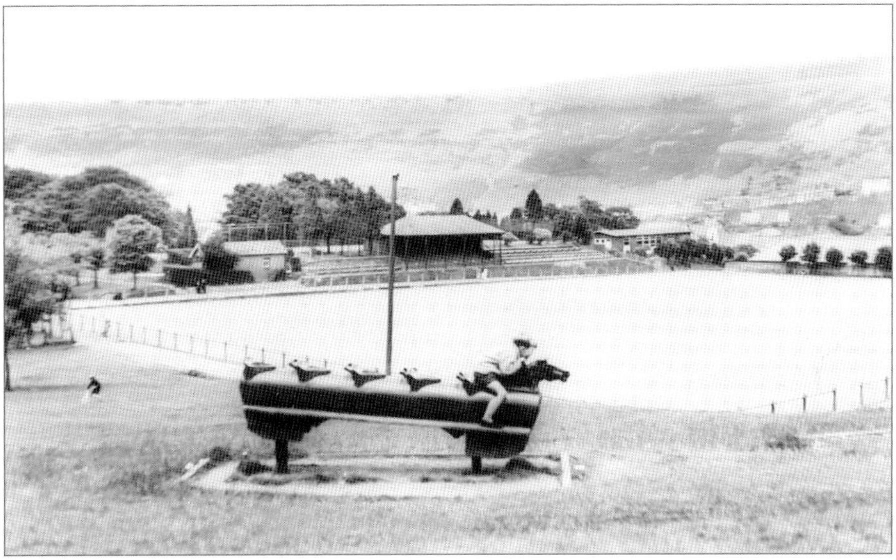

FERNDALE
Darran Park Playground c1955
F123009

One of Ferndale's most famous sons was the actor Stanley Baker, born in the town in 1927 and particularly famous for his roles in the films 'The Cruel Sea', 'The Guns of Navarone' and 'Zulu'.

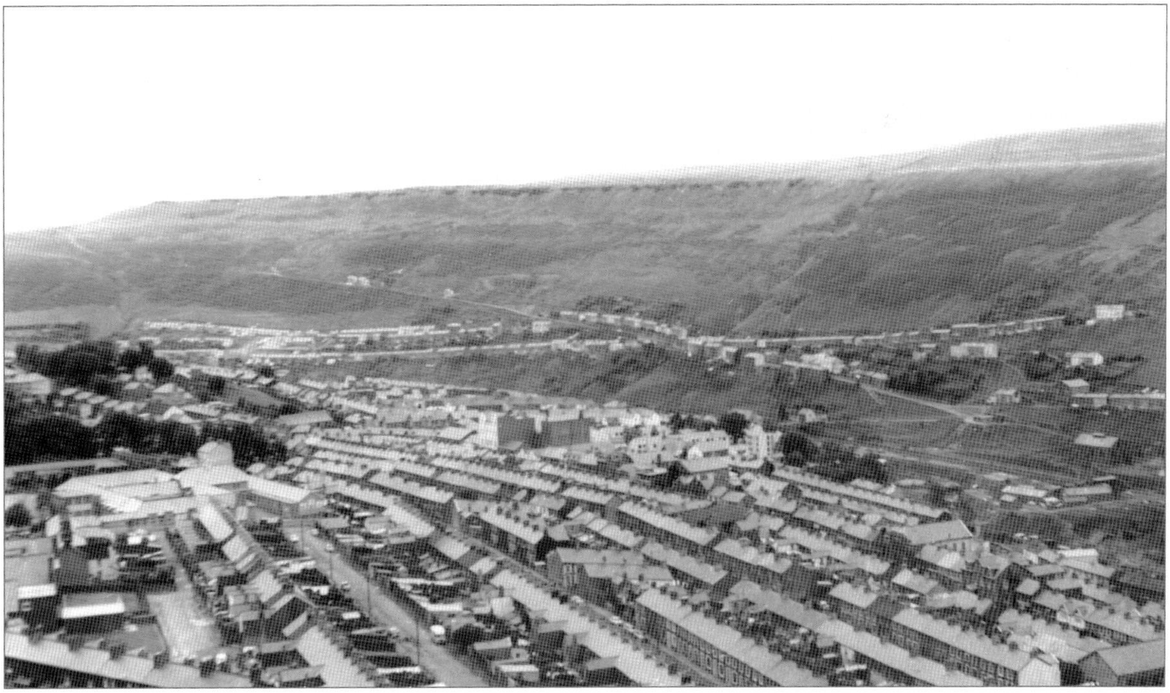

FERNDALE *and Blaenllechau c1955* F123005

In 1988 a memorial was erected close to where Ferndale No 1 and No 5 pits once stood, which commemorates 'those miners who worked, or were killed or injured, in the four Ferndale pits. Including the 231 miners who lost their lives in two frightful explosions at No 1 pit in 1867 and 1869'. Ferndale No 1 pit claimed the lives of more miners than any other coal mine in the Rhondda.

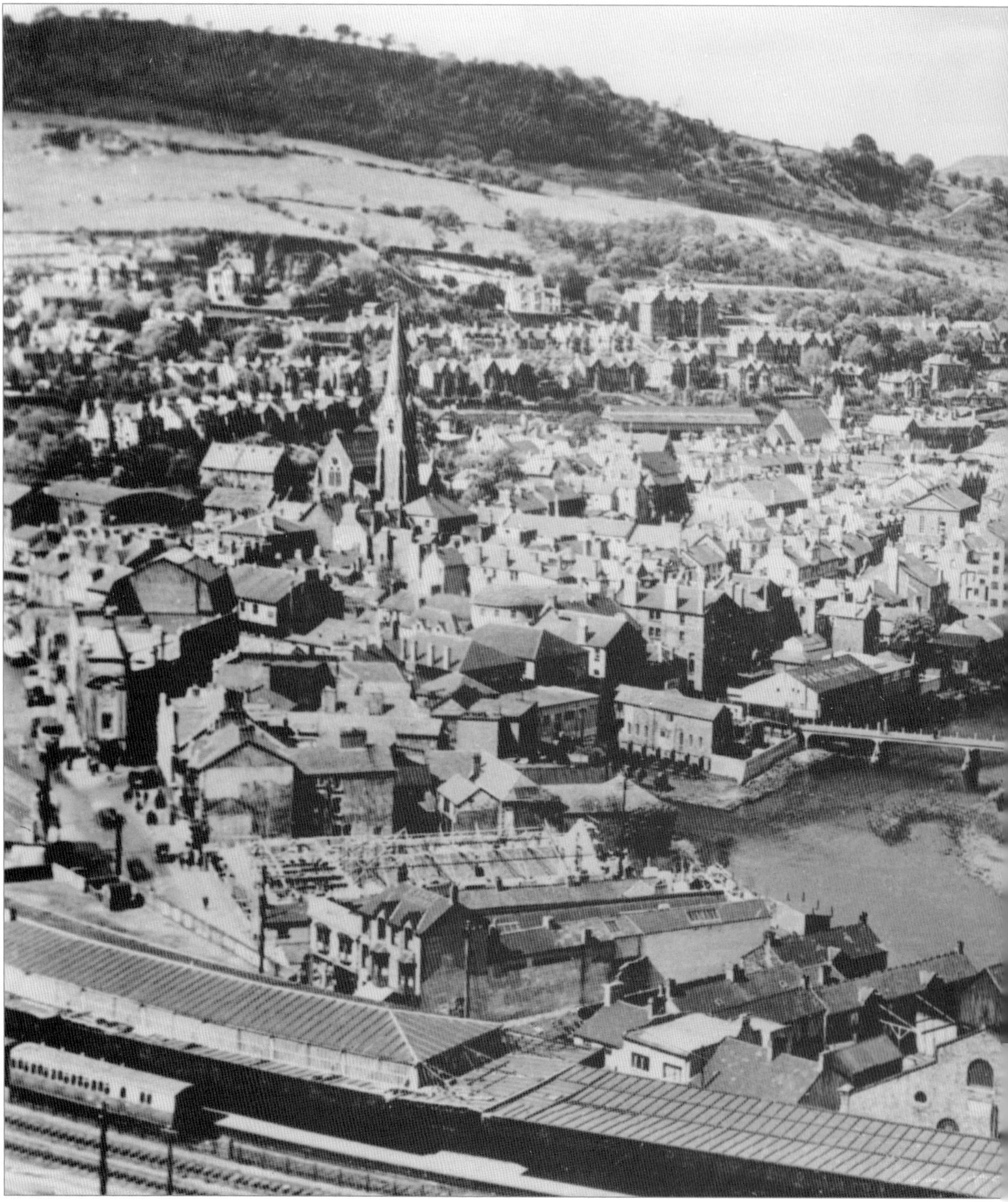

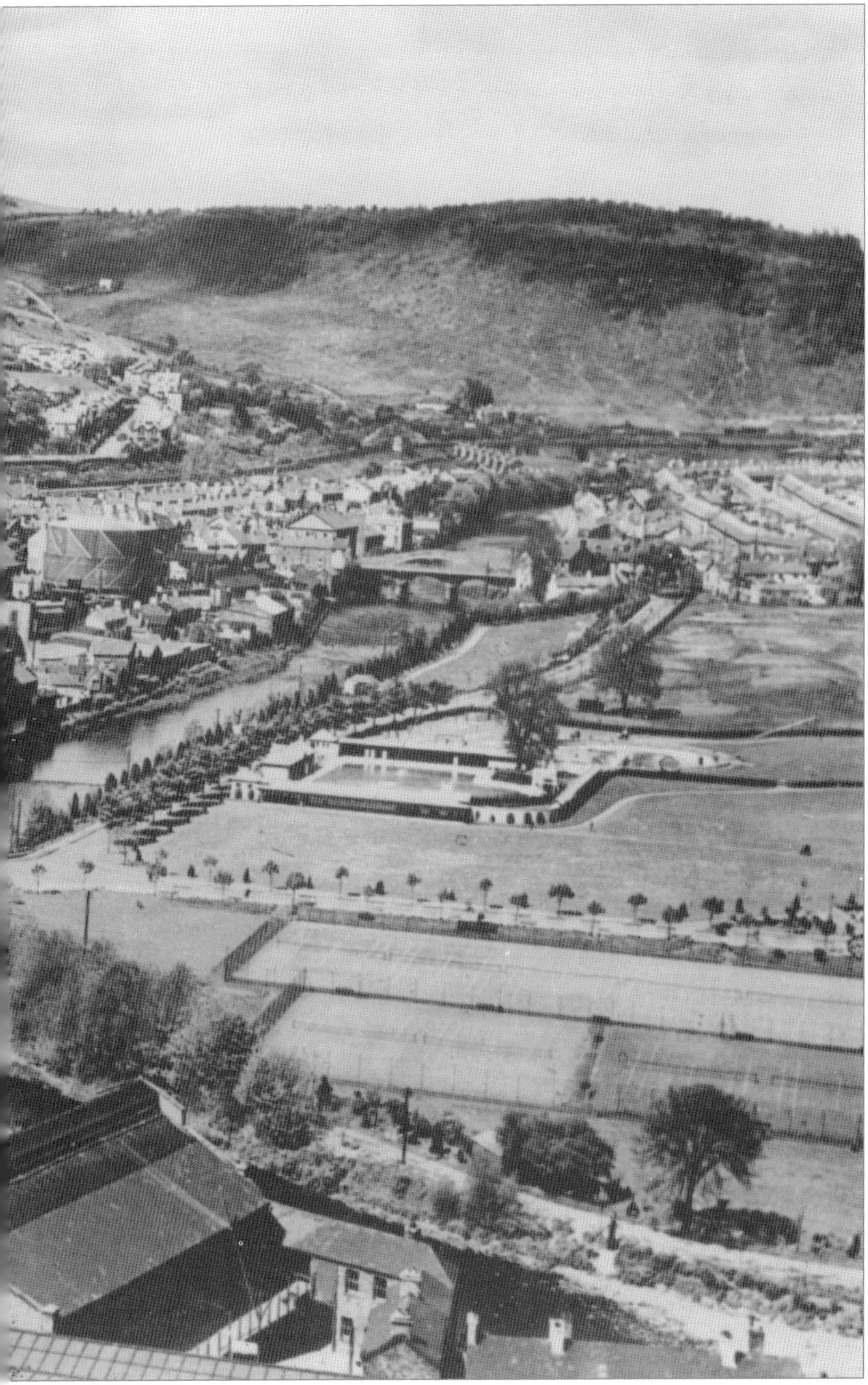

PONTYPRIDD
View from the Graig c1925 P716001

This view was taken from the heights of the 'Graig' mountain. The River Taff swings round a bend in the foreground, to merge with the very end of the Rhondda by the present 'Marks and Spencer' store. The main development in housing and commerce is on the left bank, whereas across the river was reserved for recreation. The church spire visible to the centre left is that of St Catherine's.

PONTYPRIDD, *The Old Bridge c1965* P716041

The old bridge is something of a 'folly', a quirky arched bridge of 1775 that was once the longest single-span stone bridge in Europe. It was built by an amateur stonemason, William Edwards, whose three previous efforts had all crumbled into the river. Finally, he succeeded by designing three large holes in the side, so reducing the weight of the abutments and stabilising the arch. Unfortunately the bridge proved impracticable, as it was so steep that it was difficult to get carts across, and in 1857 a new bridge, the Victoria Bridge, was built next to it.

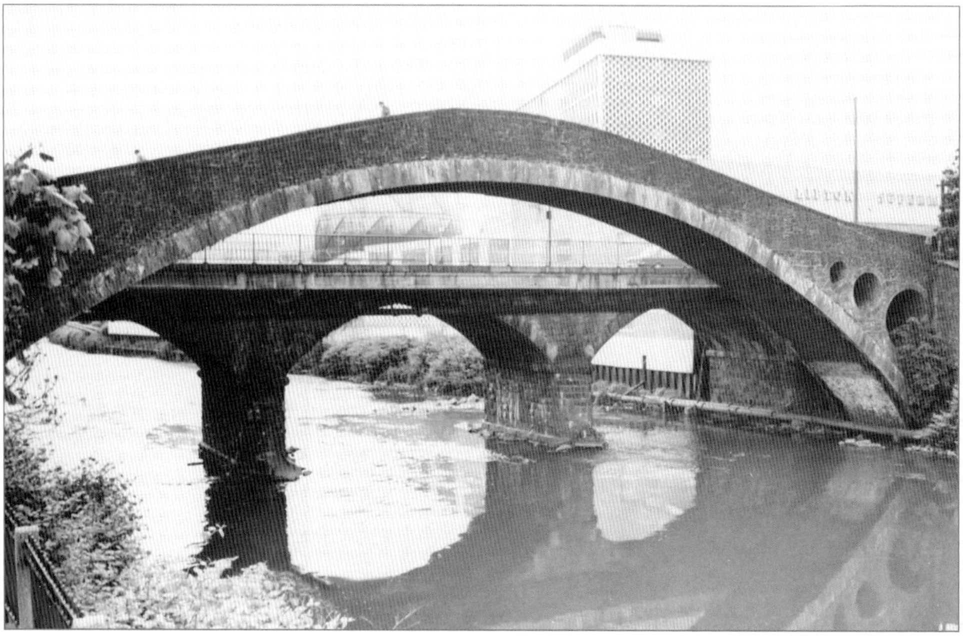

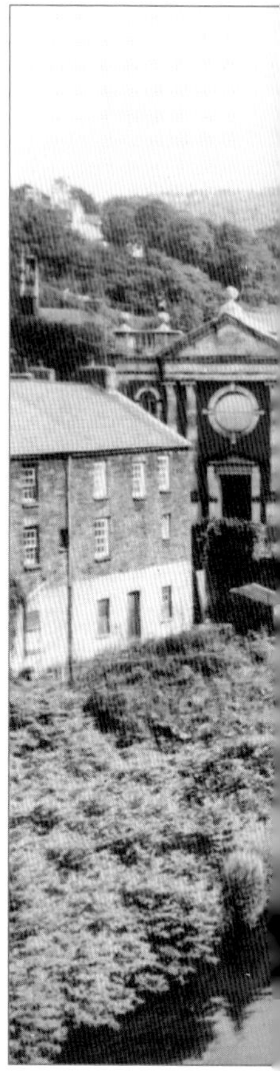

PONTYPRIDD
View from the Old Bridge c1960 P716020

Pride of place in this photograph, other than to a very large car park, goes to Pontypridd's gasometer! From the ridiculous to the sublime, the church with spire, seen right of the gas works, is St Catherine's.

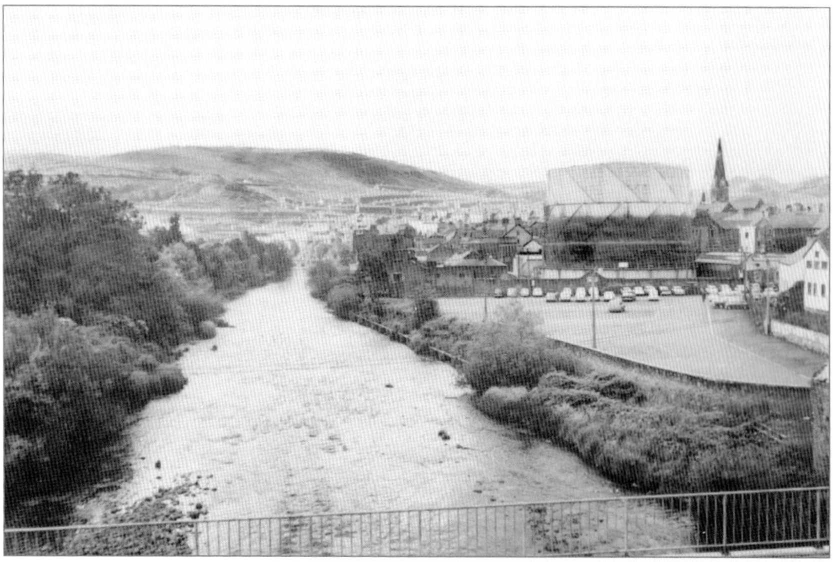

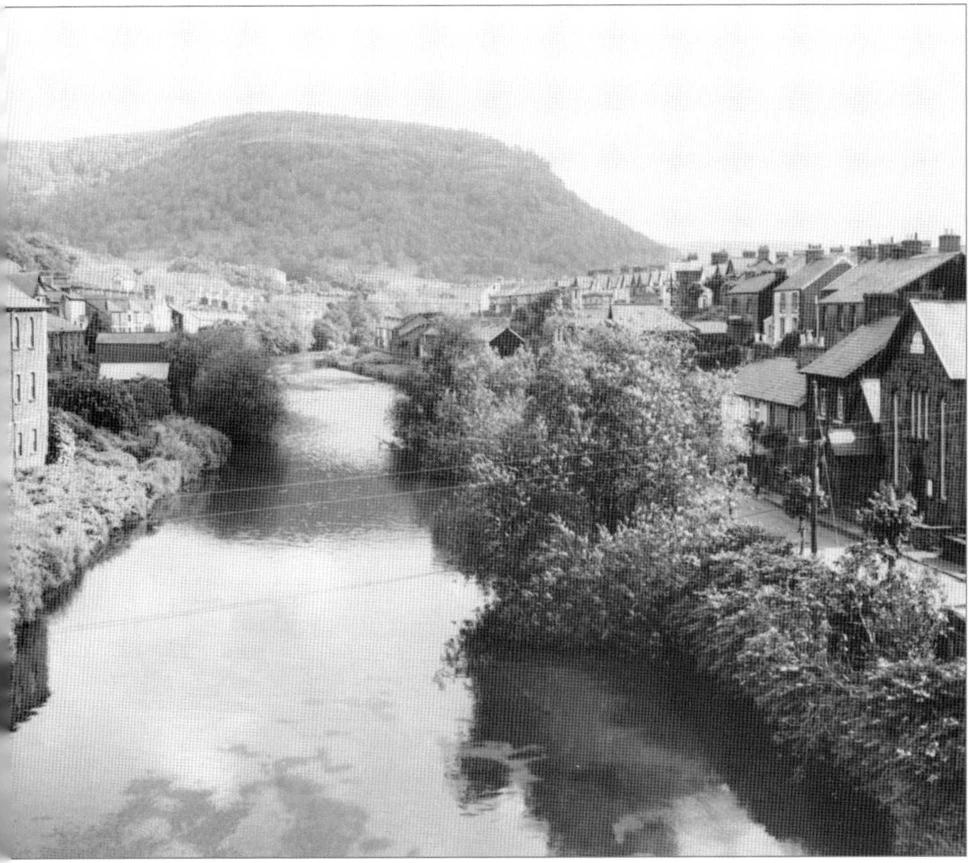

◄ **PONTYPRIDD**
View from the Old Bridge c1960
P716021

Looking upstream, the river is smooth and slow with the undergrowth creeping down to the water. There is development on both sides here with the residential buildings primarily on the right. The somewhat ornate Georgian three storey building on the left is Capel Eglwys Bach, named after the North Wales birthplace of its minister, the Rev John Evans. The building is now the Eglwysbach Medical Practice.

► **PONTYPRIDD**
The Valley from the Common c1960
P716018

The Common is one part of many parks and open places that abound in this town. It is so typical of all the Rhondda Valley towns with the surrounding mountains squeezing the houses into rows that are forced to run along the valley floor.

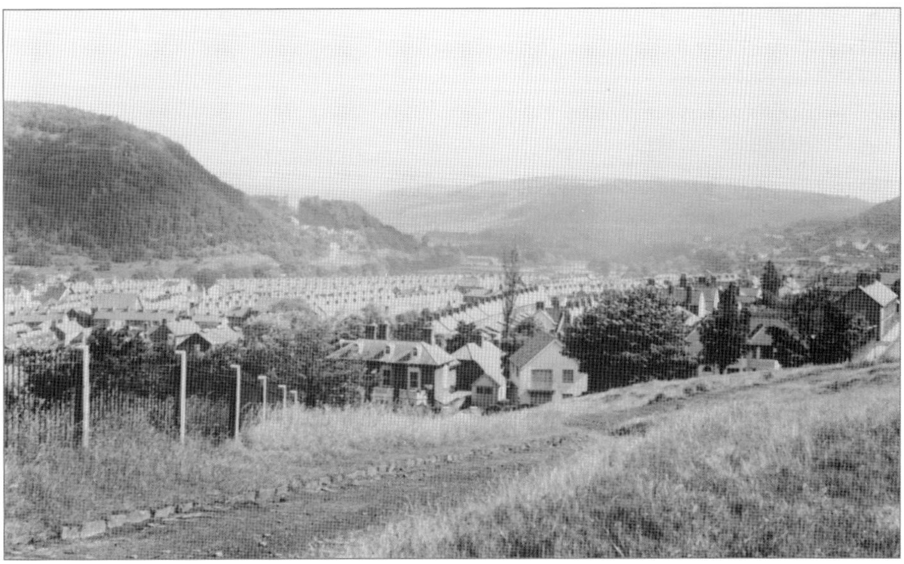

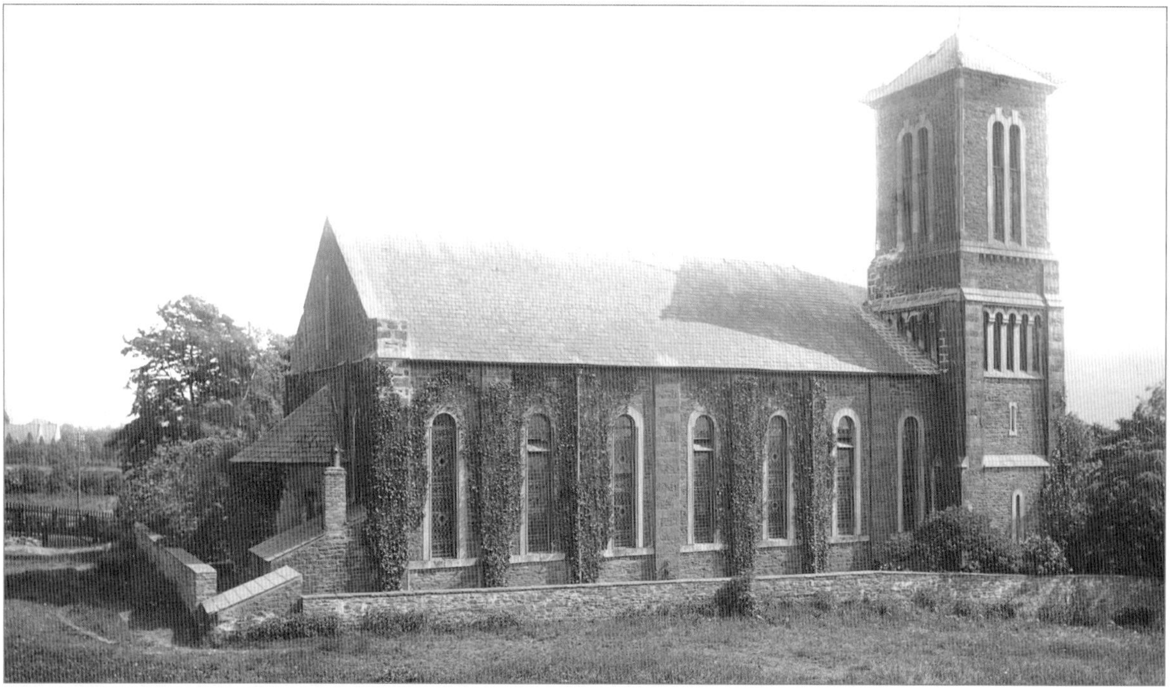

▲ **PONTYPRIDD**
Glyntaff Church 1899 43615

A mile out of the town the church was built in a charmingly simple style with neither tower nor spire but a 'square turret'. Otherwise known as St Mary's, it was built by local men around 1858, the natural ivy revealing the damp weather and clean air of the time. To encourage his own 'flock' the Rev John Griffiths established a market day each Wednesday and a special cattle fair on Easter Monday.

► **PONTYPRIDD**
Glyntaff Crematorium 1899 43619

Glyntaff cemetery opened in 1874. Although the spire with weather vane a-top might look impressive its use was more mundane - it functioned as a chimney when the crematorium opened in 1924 - the first in Wales.

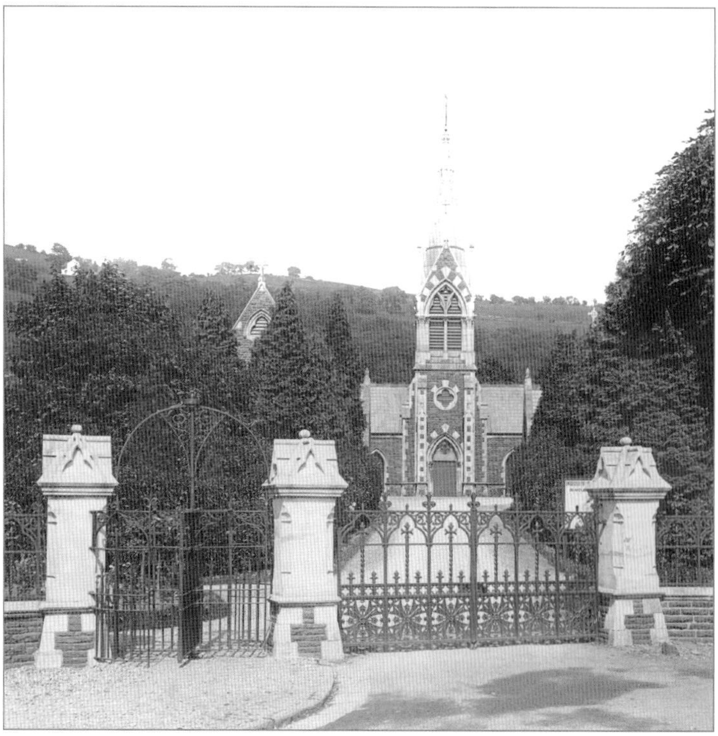

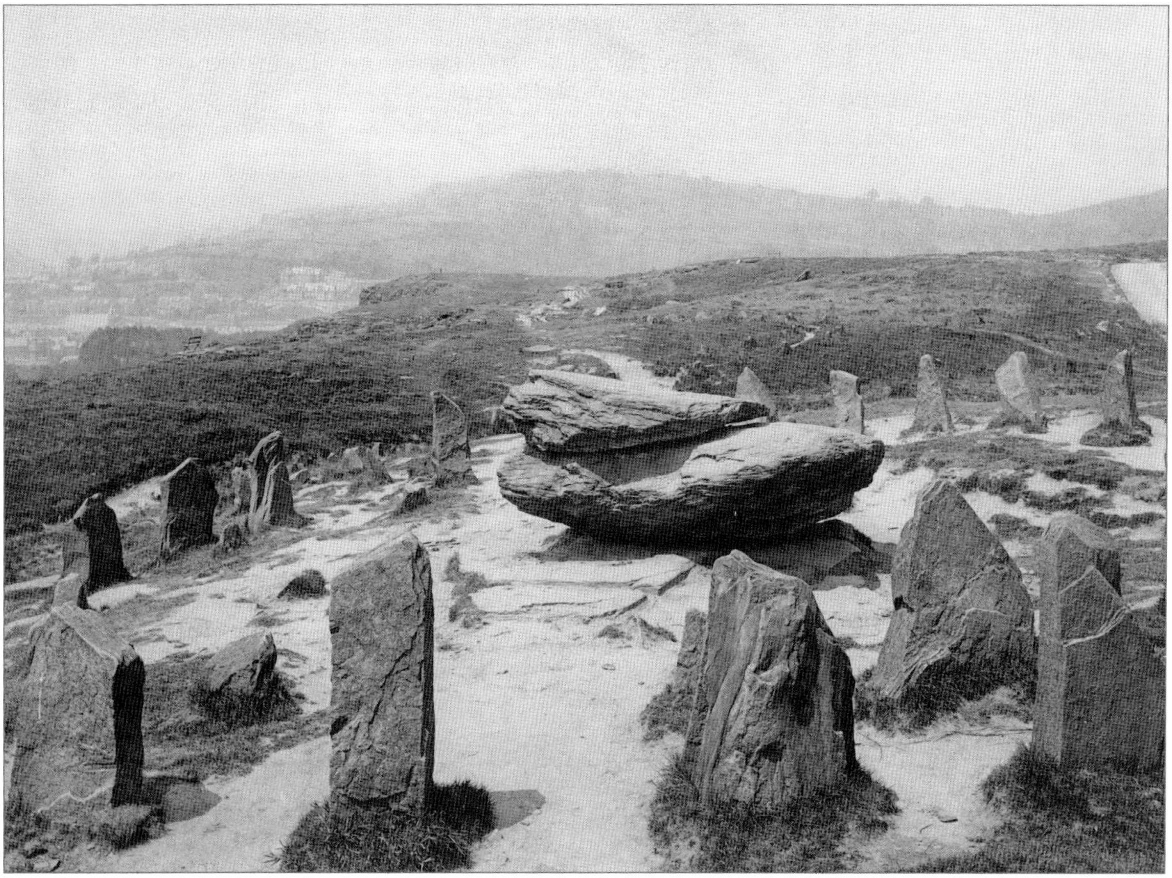

PONTYPRIDD
The Rocking Stone 1899 43620

Ancient stone circles date back to prehistoric times, when they were probably used for ceremonial and ritual purposes, and possibly had some sort of astronomical function. As we have seen, take care with Welsh stone circles - some are genuinely ancient, but many are more recent. This is a modern circle, laid out as a serpent c1860 around the huge granite 'rocking stone' left by a retreating glacier.

PONTYPRIDD
The Fountain c1955
P716006

The centrepiece is the Victorian fountain given to the town by Sir Alfred Thomas, the MP for East Glamorgan, in 1895. This was an attempt to supply the inhabitants of the town and their horses with clean drinking water from the troughs at ground level. It is topped off with the two Welsh dragons holding a canopied light aloft. It became a 'lavatory' in later life, and, more recently, the dragons were stolen!

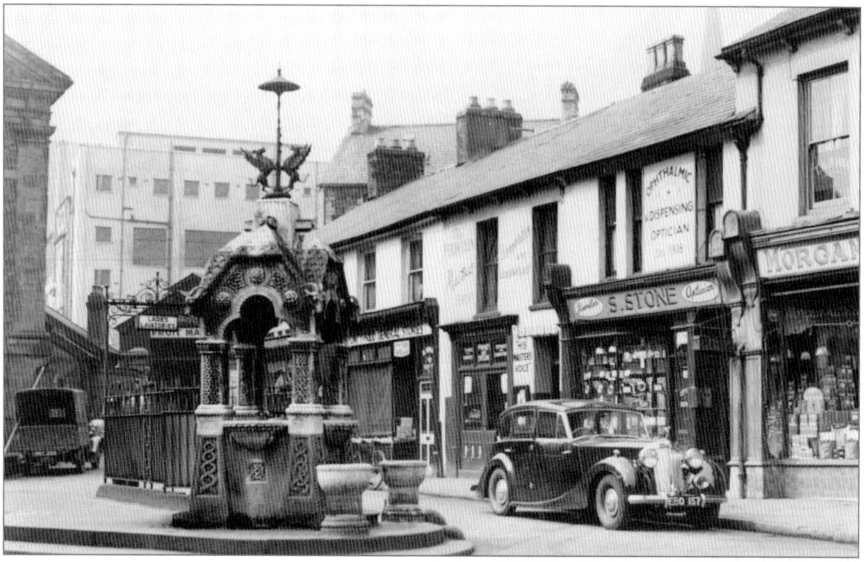

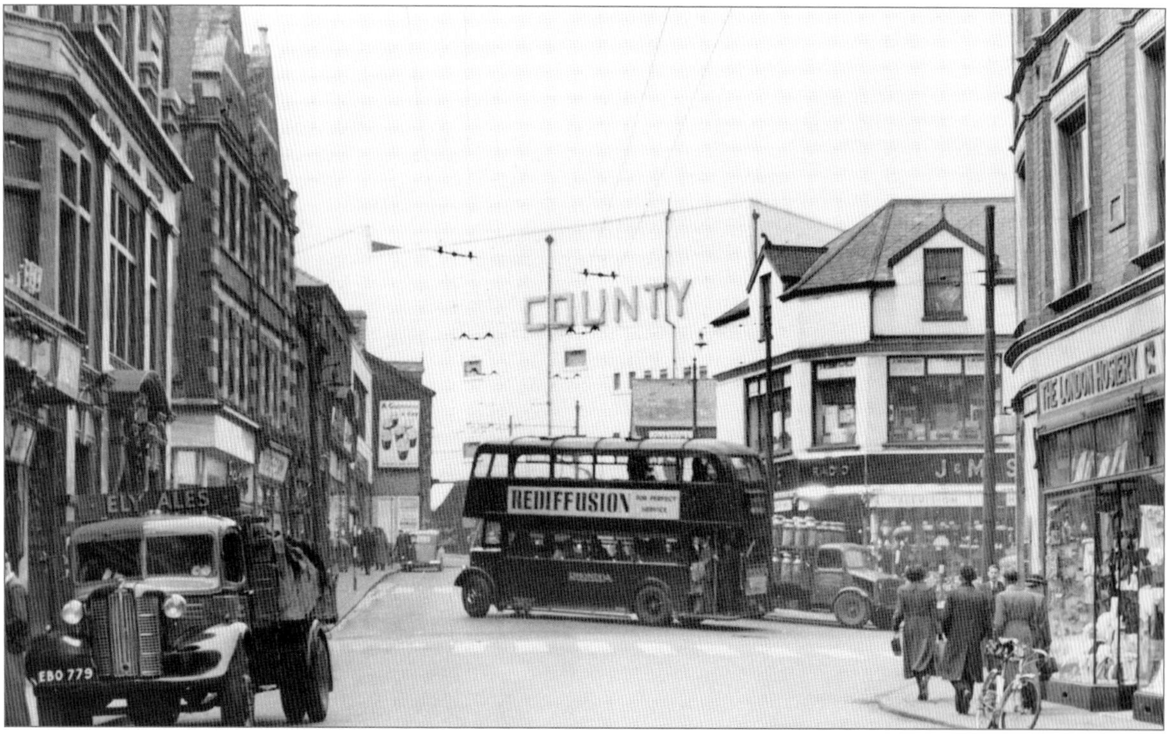

PONTYPRIDD, *Taff Street 1952* P716007

The old and the new jostle in the street at this date. The double decker bus is relatively new whereas the wagon delivering milk just behind it looks like an ex-army truck. The dray wagon for 'Ely Ales' is no youngster with its prominent 'bull-nose'. Like so many small independents the brewery closed soon after this picture was taken.

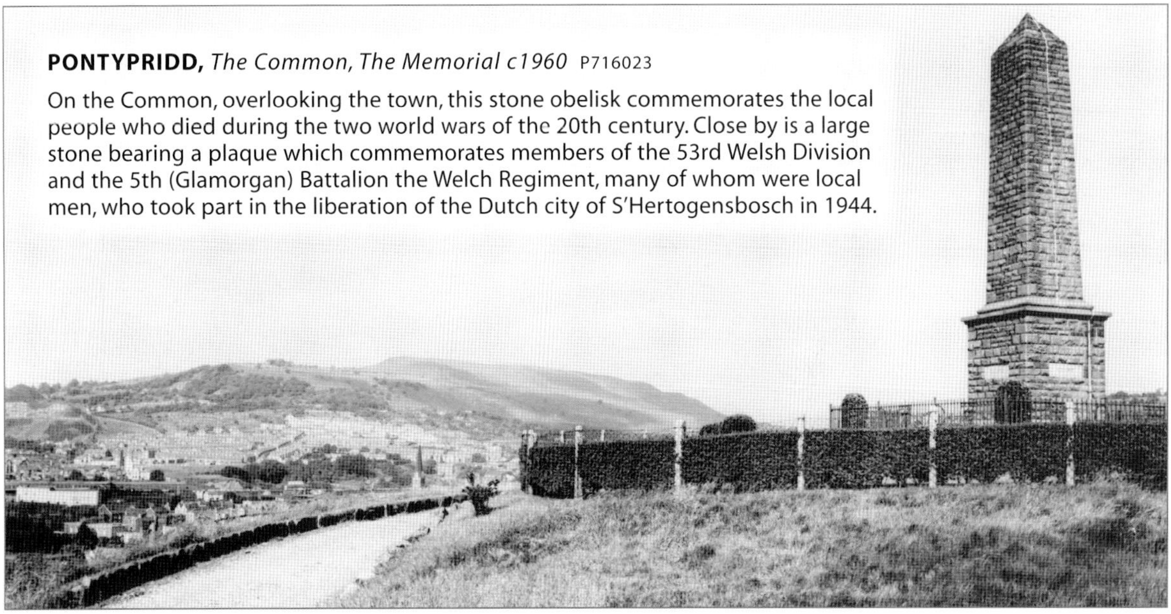

PONTYPRIDD, *The Common, The Memorial c1960* P716023

On the Common, overlooking the town, this stone obelisk commemorates the local people who died during the two world wars of the 20th century. Close by is a large stone bearing a plaque which commemorates members of the 53rd Welsh Division and the 5th (Glamorgan) Battalion the Welch Regiment, many of whom were local men, who took part in the liberation of the Dutch city of S'Hertogensbosch in 1944.

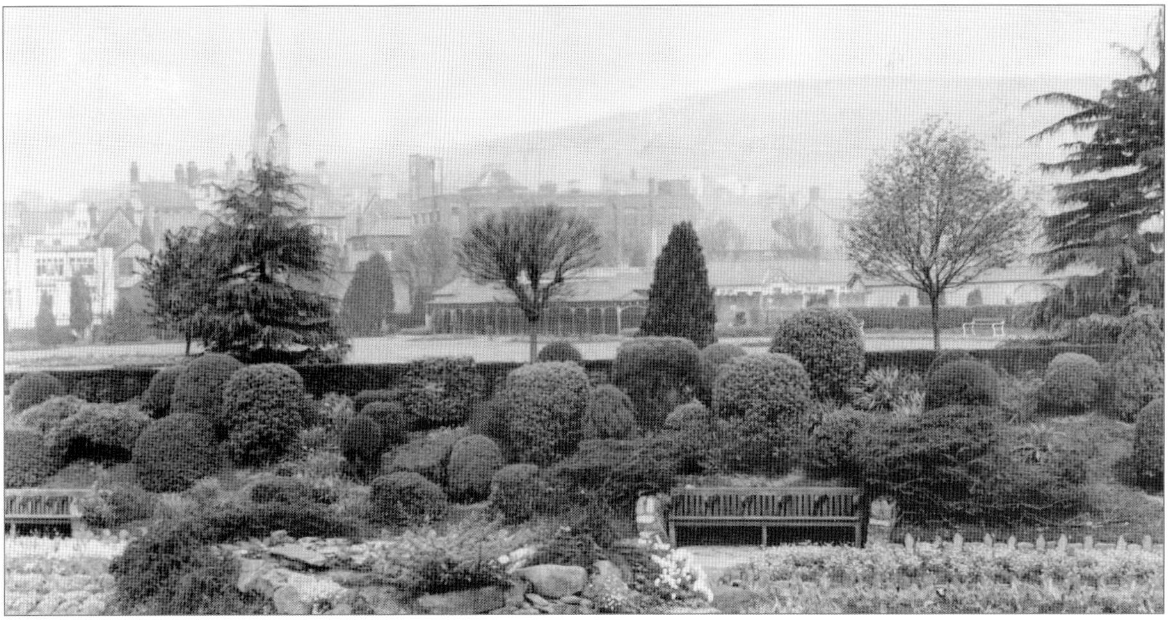

PONTYPRIDD, *Ynysangharad Park c1955* P716009

Ynysangharad Park was opened in 1923. The land was purchased by public subscription and grants from the Miners' Welfare Fund, and the park was conceived as a War Memorial for the town. Much of the park was earmarked for pleasant gardens where one could just sit and watch the world go by. In front of the bench rises a flower-bedecked rockery, whilst to the rear is a multitude of well-trimmed shrubbery. Appearing again in the distance is the spire of St Catherine's.

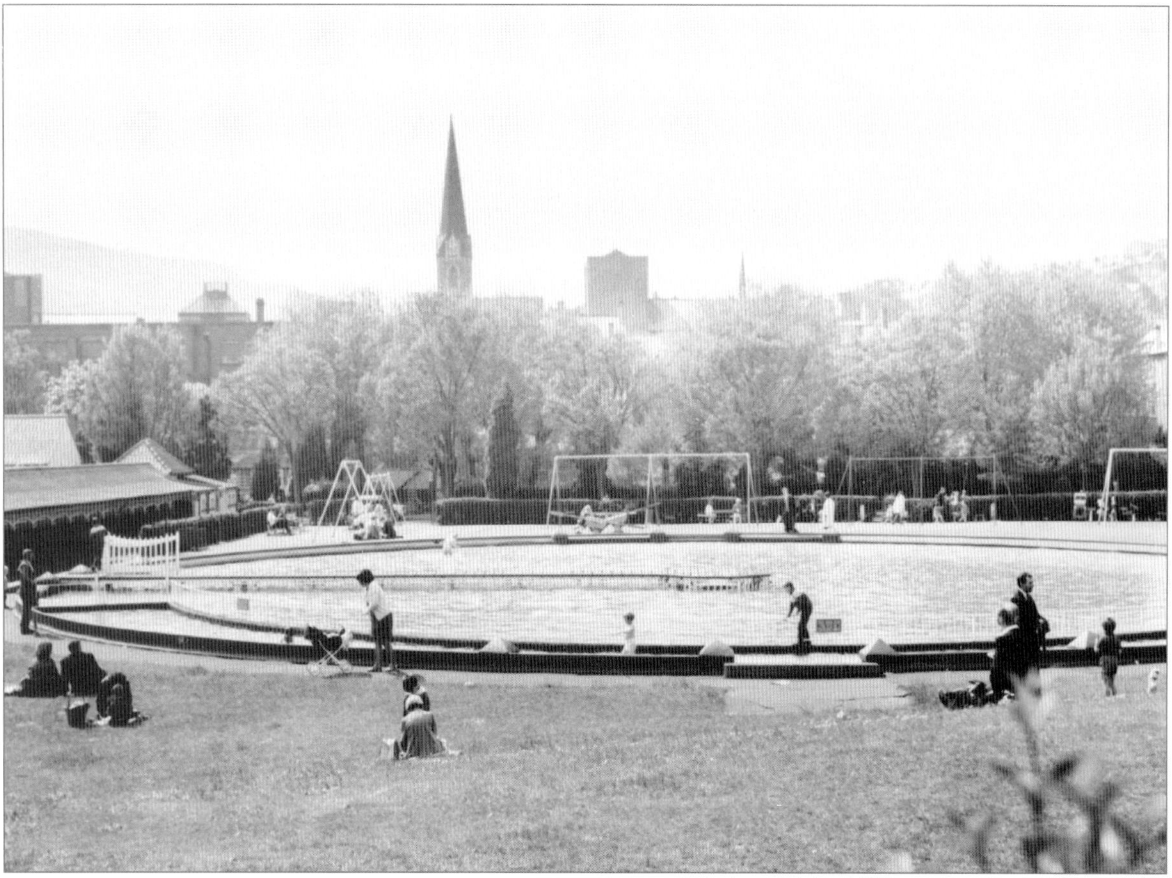

PONTYPRIDD

Ynysangharad Park c1960 P716046

This is a view of the park with plenty of activity around the paddling pool, but with no one in it. It could well have been too early in the year as the people on the grass look well covered up; additionally the trees are not yet in full leaf. The ubiquitous St Catherine breaks through what would have been the skyline.

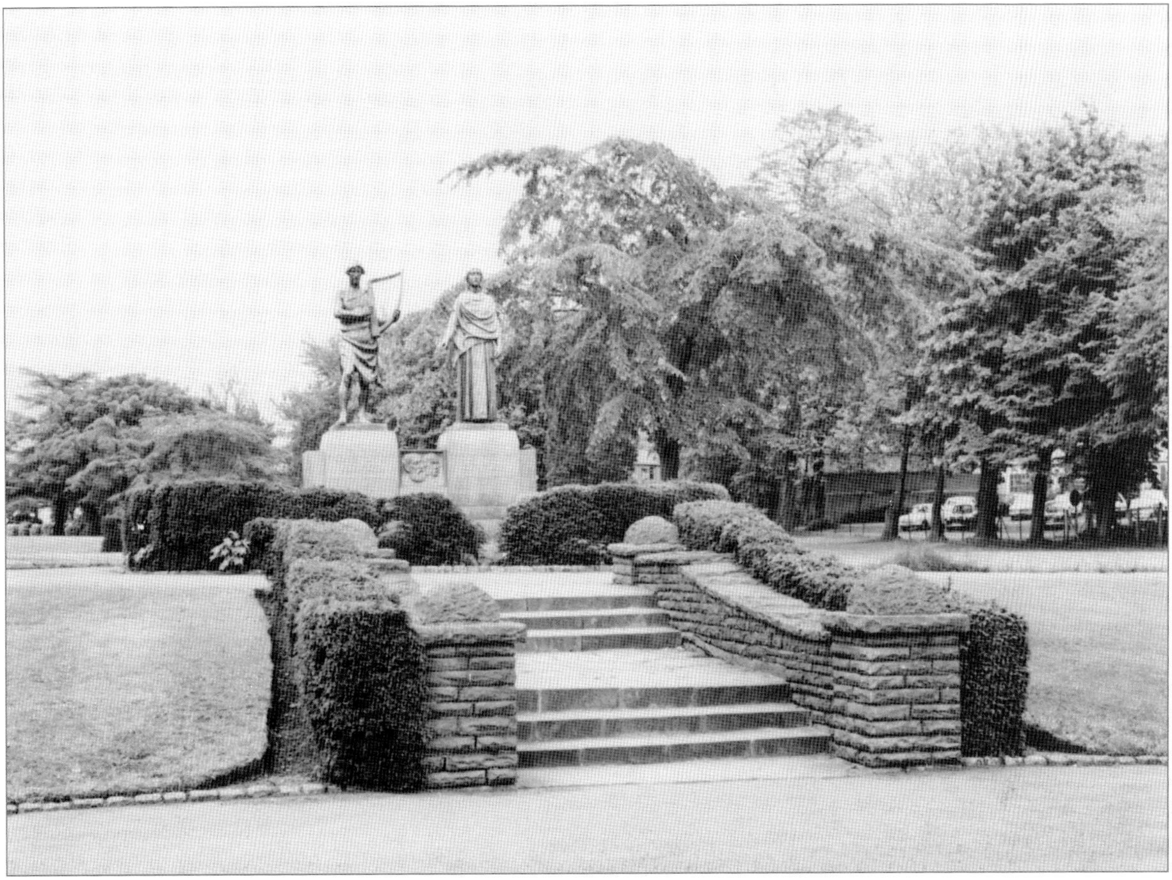

PONTYPRIDD

Ynysangharad Park, The Memorial c1960 P716043

This memorial is to a very famous Welsh couple, Evan and James James, who were the father and son team who wrote the Welsh National Anthem, 'Land of my Fathers'. Evan wrote the words in 1856 and James composed the tune, which is based on an old harp melody.

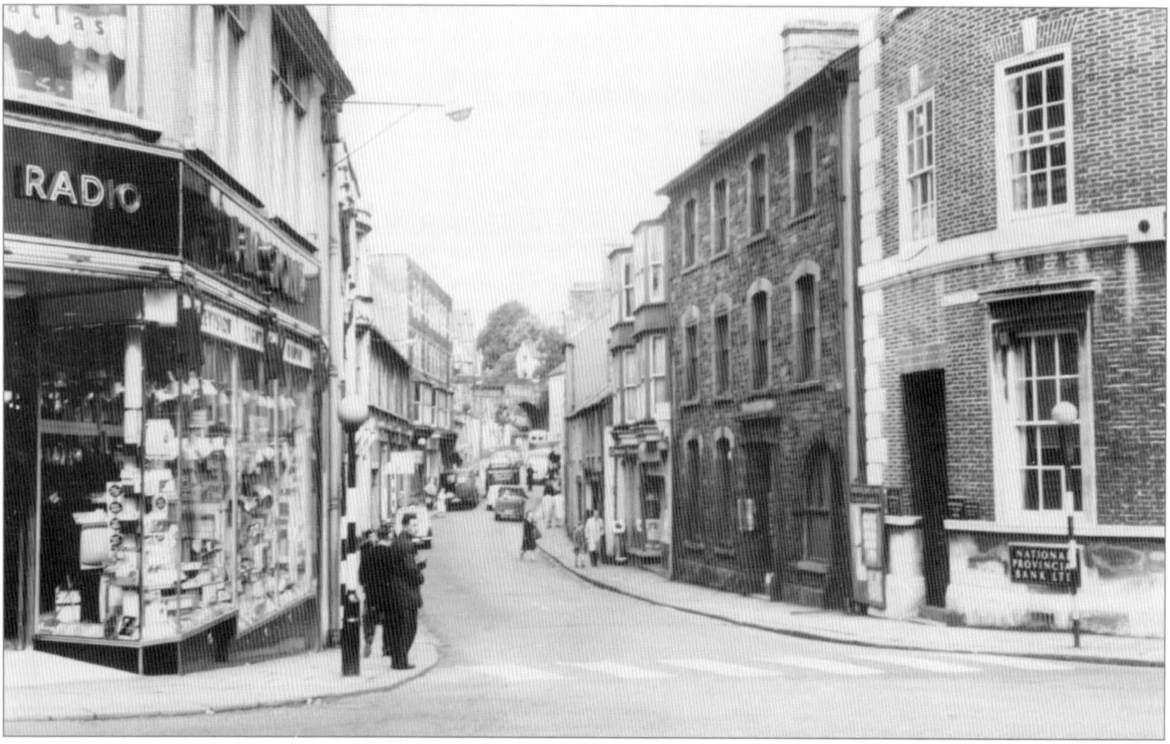

PONTYPRIDD

Mill Street c1955 P716019

The National Provincial Bank leads us into Mill Street but this is the final photograph and a fitting way to end. For this was the very street where Evan James, a weaver from Pontypridd, wrote the words one Sunday morning in 1856 to 'Hen Wlad fy Nhadau'. Known throughout the world as 'Land of my Fathers' his son James James composed the tune a year later. It was given prominence at the National Eisteddfod held at Bangor in 1874, and since that date has been considered the song which, more than any other, expresses the Welsh national sentiment.

It is now afforded official status as the National Anthem of Wales.

The land of my fathers is dear to me,
A land of poets and minstrels, famed men.
Her brave warriors, patriots most blessed,
It was for freedom that they lost their blood.

Homeland! I am devoted to my country;
So long as the sea is a wall
to this fair beautiful land
May the ancient language remain.

INDEX

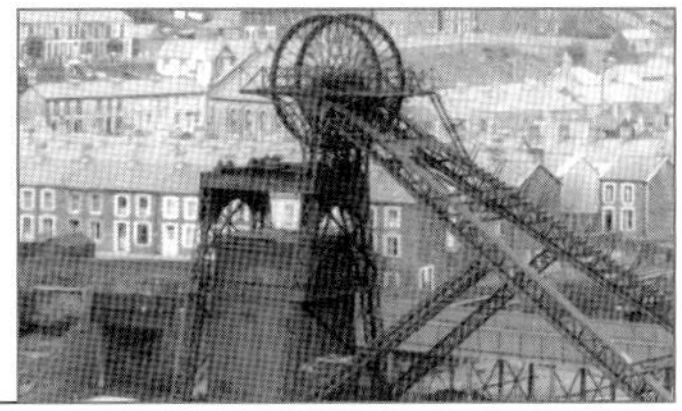

The Francis Frith Collection Titles

www.francisfrith.com

The Francis Frith Collection publishes over 100 new titles each year. A selection of those currently available is listed below. For latest catalogue please contact The Francis Frith Collection.
Town Books 96 pages, approximately 75 photos. ***County and Themed Books*** 128 pages, approximately 135 photos (unless specified). Pocket Albums are miniature editions of Frith local history books 128 pages, approximately 95 photos.

Accrington Old and New
Alderley Edge and Wilmslow
Amersham, Chesham and Rickmansworth
Andover
Around Abergavenny
Around Alton
Aylesbury
Barnstaple
Bedford
Bedfordshire
Berkshire Living Memories
Berkshire Pocket Album
Blackpool Pocket Album
Bognor Regis
Bournemouth
Bradford
Bridgend
Bridport
Brighton and Hove
Bristol
Buckinghamshire
Calne Living Memories
Camberley Pocket Album
Canterbury Cathedral
Cardiff Old and New
Chatham and the Medway Towns
Chelmsford
Chepstow Then and Now
Cheshire
Cheshire Living Memories
Chester
Chesterfield
Chigwell
Christchurch
Churches of East Cornwall
Clevedon
Clitheroe
Corby Living Memories
Cornish Coast
Cornwall Living Memories
Cotswold Living Memories
Cotswold Pocket Album
Coulsdon, Chipstead and Woodmanstern
County Durham
Cromer, Sheringham and Holt
Dartmoor Pocket Album
Derby
Derbyshire
Derbyshire Living Memories
Devon
Devon Churches
Dorchester
Dorset Coast Pocket Album
Dorset Living Memories
Dorset Villages
Down the Dart
Down the Severn
Down the Thames
Dunmow, Thaxted and Finchingfield
Durham
East Anglia Pocket Album
East Devon
East Grinstead
Edinburgh
Ely and The Fens
Essex Pocket Album
Essex Second Selection
Essex: The London Boroughs
Exeter
Exmoor
Falmouth
Farnborough, Fleet and Aldershot
Folkestone
Frome
Furness and Cartmel Peninsulas
Glamorgan
Glasgow
Glastonbury
Gloucester
Gloucestershire
Greater Manchester
Guildford
Hailsham
Hampshire
Harrogate
Hastings and Bexhill
Haywards Heath Living Memories
Heads of the Valleys
Heart of Lancashire Pocket Album
Helston
Herefordshire
Horsham
Humberside Pocket Album
Huntingdon, St Neots and St Ives
Hythe, Romney Marsh and Ashford
Ilfracombe
Ipswich Pocket Album
Isle of Wight
Isle of Wight Living Memories
King's Lynn
Kingston upon Thames
Lake District Pocket Album
Lancashire Living Memories
Lancashire Villages

Available from your local bookshop or from the publisher

The Francis Frith Collection Titles (continued)

Lancaster, Morecambe and Heysham Pocket Album
Leeds Pocket Album
Leicester
Leicestershire
Lincolnshire Living Memoires
Lincolnshire Pocket Album
Liverpool and Merseyside
London Pocket Album
Ludlow
Maidenhead
Maidstone
Malmesbury
Manchester Pocket Album
Marlborough
Matlock
Merseyside Living Memories
Nantwich and Crewe
New Forest
Newbury Living Memories
Newquay to St Ives
North Devon Living Memories
North London
North Wales
North Yorkshire
Northamptonshire
Northumberland
Northwich
Nottingham
Nottinghamshire Pocket Album
Oakham
Odiham Then and Now
Oxford Pocket Album
Oxfordshire
Padstow
Pembrokeshire
Penzance
Petersfield Then and Now
Plymouth
Poole and Sandbanks
Preston Pocket Album
Ramsgate Old and New
Reading Pocket Album
Redditch Living Memories
Redhill to Reigate
Richmond
Ringwood
Rochdale
Romford Pocket Album
Salisbury Pocket Album
Scotland
Scottish Castles
Sevenoaks and Tonbridge
Sheffield and South Yorkshire Pocket Album
Shropshire
Somerset
South Devon Coast
South Devon Living Memories
South East London
Southampton Pocket Album
Southend Pocket Album
Southport
Southwold to Aldeburgh
Stourbridge Living Memories
Stratford upon Avon
Stroud
Suffolk
Suffolk Pocket Album
Surrey Living Memories
Sussex
Sutton
Swanage and Purbeck
Swansea Pocket Album
Swindon Living Memories
Taunton
Teignmouth
Tenby and Saundersfoot
Tiverton
Torbay
Truro
Uppingham
Villages of Kent
Villages of Surrey
Villages of Sussex Pocket Album
Wakefield and the Five Towns Living Memories
Warrington
Warwick
Warwickshire Pocket Album
Wellingborough Living Memories
Wells
Welsh Castles
West Midlands Pocket Album
West Wiltshire Towns
West Yorkshire
Weston-super-Mare
Weymouth
Widnes and Runcorn
Wiltshire Churches
Wiltshire Living Memories
Wiltshire Pocket Album
Wimborne
Winchester Pocket Album
Windermere
Windsor
Wirral
Wokingham and Bracknell
Woodbridge
Worcester
Worcestershire
Worcestershire Living Memories
Wyre Forest
York Pocket Album
Yorkshire
Yorkshire Coastal Memories
Yorkshire Dales
Yorkshire Revisited

FRITH PRODUCTS & SERVICES

Francis Frith would doubtless be pleased to know that the pioneering publishing venture he started in 1860 still continues today. Over a hundred and forty years later, The Francis Frith Collection continues in the same innovative tradition and is now one of the foremost publishers of vintage photographs in the world. Some of the current activities include:

INTERIOR DECORATION

Today Frith's photographs can be seen framed and as giant wall murals in thousands of pubs, restaurants, hotels, banks, retail stores and other public buildings throughout the country. In every case they enhance the unique local atmosphere of the places they depict and provide reminders of gentler days in an increasingly busy and frenetic world.

PRODUCT PROMOTIONS

Frith products are used by many major companies to promote the sales of their own products or to reinforce their own history and heritage. Frith promotions have been used by Hovis bread, Courage beers, Scots Porage Oats, Colman's mustard, Cadbury's foods, Mellow Birds coffee, Dunhill pipe tobacco, Guinness, and Bulmer's Cider.

GENEALOGY AND FAMILY HISTORY

As the interest in family history and roots grows world-wide, more and more people are turning to Frith's photographs of Great Britain for images of the towns, villages and streets where their ancestors lived; and, of course, photographs of the churches and chapels where their ancestors were christened, married and buried are an essential part of every genealogy tree and family album.

FRITH PRODUCTS

All Frith photographs are available Framed or just as Mounted Prints and Posters (size 23 x 16 inches). These may be ordered from the address below. Other products available are- Address Books, Calendars, Jigsaws, Canvas Prints, Notelets and local and prestige books.

THE INTERNET

Already ninety thousand Frith photographs can be viewed and purchased on the internet through the Frith websites and a myriad of partner sites.

For more detailed information on Frith companies and products, look at this site:
www.francisfrith.com

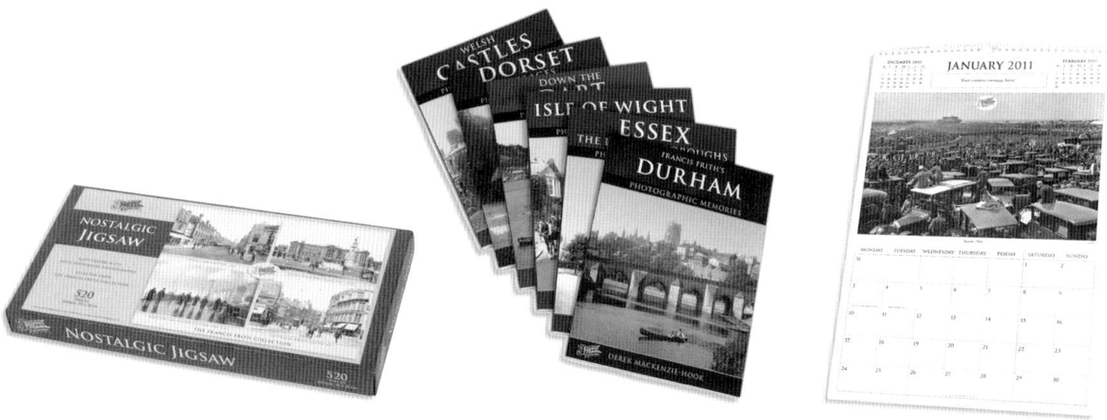

See the complete list of Frith Books at: www.francisfrith.com
This web site is regularly updated with the latest list of publications from The Francis Frith Collection. If you wish to buy books relating to another part of the country that your local bookshop does not stock, you may purchase on-line.

For further information, trade, or author enquiries please contact us at the address below:
The Francis Frith Collection, Unit 6, Oakley Business Park, Wylye Road, Dinton, Wiltshire SP3 5EU.
Tel: +44 (0)1722 716 376 Fax: +44 (0)1722 716 881 Email: sales@francisfrith.co.uk

See Frith products on the internet at www.francisfrith.com

FREE PRINT OF YOUR CHOICE

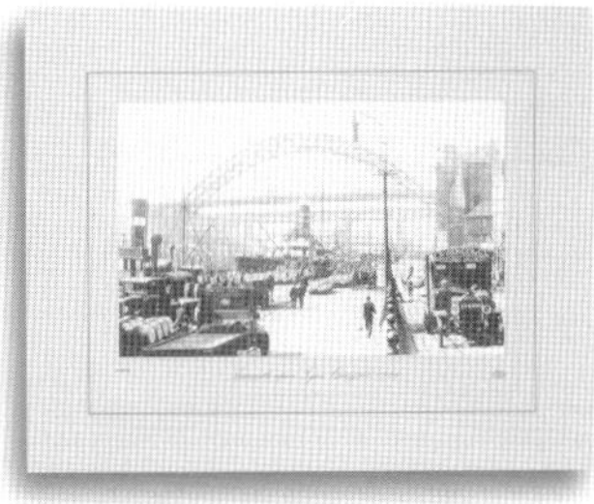

Mounted Print
Overall size 14 x 11 inches (355 x 280mm)

Choose any Frith photograph in this book. Simply complete the Voucher opposite and return it with your remittance for £3.50 (to cover postage and handling) and we will print the photograph of your choice in SEPIA (size 11 x 8 inches) and supply it in a cream mount with a burgundy rule line (overall size 14 x 11 inches). **Please note: aerial photographs and photographs with a reference number starting with a "Z" are not Frith photographs and cannot be supplied under this offer. Offer valid for delivery to one UK address only**.

***PLUS:* Order additional Mounted Prints at HALF PRICE - £9.50 each** (normally £19.00)
If you would like to order more Frith prints from this book, possibly as gifts for friends and family, you can buy them at half price (with no additional postage and handling costs).

***PLUS:* Have your Mounted Prints framed**
For an extra £18.00 per print you can have your mounted print(s) framed in an elegant polished wood and gilt moulding, overall size 16 x 13 inches (no additional postage and handling required).

IMPORTANT!

These special prices are only available if you use this form to order. You must use the ORIGINAL VOUCHER on this page (no copies permitted). We can only despatch to one UK address. This offer cannot be combined with any other offer.

Send completed Voucher form to:
The Francis Frith Collection, Unit 6, Oakley Business Park, Wylye Road, Dinton, Wiltshire SP3 5EU

CHOOSE A PHOTOGRAPH FROM THIS BOOK

Voucher *for* **FREE** *and Reduced Price Frith Prints*

Please do not photocopy this voucher. Only the original is valid, so please fill it in, cut it out and return it to us with your order.

Picture ref no	Page no	Qty	Mounted @ £9.50	Framed + £18.00	Total Cost £
		1	Free of charge*	£	£
			£9.50	£	£
			£9.50	£	£
			£9.50	£	£
			£9.50	£	£
			£9.50	£	£
Please allow 28 days for delivery.			* Post & handling		£3.50
Offer available to one UK address only			Total Order Cost		£

Title of this book ....
I enclose a cheque/postal order for £ ....
made payable to 'The Francis Frith Collection'

OR please debit my Mastercard / Visa / Maestro card, details below

Card Number:

Issue No (Maestro only): Valid from (Maestro):

Card Security Number: Expires:

Signature:

Name Mr/Mrs/Ms ....
Address ....
....
....
.... Postcode ....
Daytime Tel No ....
Email ....

978-1-84589-560-0 Valid to 31/12/12

Free Print - see overleaf

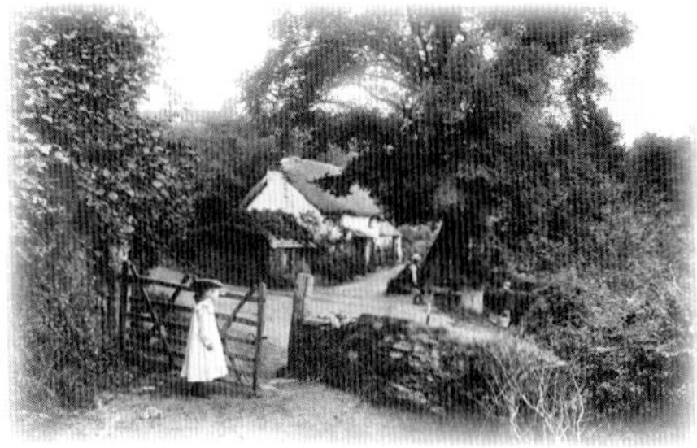

Can you help us with information about any of the Frith photographs in this book?

We are gradually compiling an historical record for each of the photographs in the Frith archive. It is always fascinating to find out the names of the people shown in the pictures, as well as insights into the shops, buildings and other features depicted.

If you recognize anyone in the photographs in this book, or if you have information not already included in the author's caption, do let us know. We would love to hear from you, and will try to publish it in future books or articles.

An Invitation from The Francis Frith Collection to Share Your Memories

The 'Share Your Memories' feature of our website allows members of the public to add personal memories relating to the places featured in our photographs, or comment on others already added. Seeing a place from your past can rekindle forgotten or long held memories. Why not visit the website, find photographs of places you know well and add YOUR story for others to read and enjoy? We would love to hear from you!

www.francisfrith.com/memories

Our production team

Frith books are produced by a small dedicated team at offices near Salisbury. Most have worked with the Frith Collection for many years. All have in common one quality: they have a passion for the Frith Collection.

Frith Books and Gifts

We have a wide range of books and gifts available on our website utilising our photographic archive, many of which can be individually personalised.

www.francisfrith.com